Teaching
READING
to
ENGLISH
LEARNERS

GRADES 6–12 | SECOND EDITION

To my most precious product and brilliant Dr. Luis Mauricio Calderón.

—Margarita

To all those who believe and inspire, past and present.
Sin ellos, todo no habría sido posible ni habría merecido la pena.

—Shawn

Teaching
READING
to
ENGLISH
LEARNERS

GRADES 6–12 | SECOND EDITION

A Framework for Improving Achievement in the Content Areas

Margarita Espino Calderón • Shawn Slakk

CORWIN
A SAGE Publishing Company

FOR INFORMATION:

Corwin

A SAGE Company

2455 Teller Road

Thousand Oaks, California 91320

(800) 233-9936

www.corwin.com

SAGE Publications Ltd.

1 Oliver's Yard

55 City Road

London EC1Y 1SP

United Kingdom

SAGE Publications India Pvt. Ltd.

B 1/I 1 Mohan Cooperative Industrial Area

Mathura Road, New Delhi 110 044

India

SAGE Publications Asia-Pacific Pte. Ltd.

3 Church Street

#10-04 Samsung Hub

Singapore 049483

Program Director: Dan Alpert

Associate Editor: Lucas Schleicher

Editorial Assistant: Mia Rodriguez

Production Editor: Amy Schroller

Copy Editor: Lana Arndt

Typesetter: Hurix Digital

Proofreader: Dennis W. Webb

Indexer: Wendy Allex

Cover Designer: Michael Dubowe

Marketing Manager: Maura Sullivan

Printed in the United States of America

Library of Congress Cataloging-in-Publication Data

Names: Calderón, Margarita Espino, author. | Slakk, Shawn, author.

Title: Teaching reading to English language learners, grades 6-12 : a framework for improving achievement in the content areas / Margarita Espino Calderón and Shawn Slakk.

Description: Second edition. | Thousand Oaks, California: Corwin, A Sage Company, [2018] | Includes bibliographical references and index.

Identifiers: LCCN 2017049687 | ISBN 9781506375748 (softcover : alk. paper)

Subjects: LCSH: English language — Study and teaching (Middle school) — Foreign speakers. | English language — Study and teaching (Secondary) — Foreign speakers. | Content area reading.

Classification: LCC PE1128.A2 C25 2018 | DDC 428.2/4–dc23

LC record available at https://lccn.loc.gov/2017049687

This book is printed on acid-free paper.

18 19 20 21 22 10 9 8 7 6 5 4 3 2 1

Contents

Preface

What We Have Learned Since the First Edition of This Book

Since the first edition appeared 10 years ago, we have worked with many more schools throughout the country, conducting long-term professional development workshops and classroom coaching. Several have been international professional development sessions. Through these experiences, we have come to realize that the basic instructional components for teaching academic language/vocabulary, reading comprehension, and academic writing cut across all subjects, grade levels, and student diversity. Invariably, teachers tell us that all students benefit. An advanced placement algebra teacher told us this spring that her students had never achieved as well until this year when she started using these strategies.

It is exciting that this original study on the essential components for helping English Learners (ELs) and their classroom peers succeed has withstood the test of time. We coached hundreds of teachers in our classroom visits, and we too learned a lot! We learned from the real masters – the math, science, social studies, language arts, and ESL/ELD teachers as they applied the instruction in diverse classrooms, making appropriate adaptations.

Soon, we began to observe certain patterns of adaptations and small tweaking. Happy to see these variations and additions, we now want to share ways to enhance the original instructional strategies and yet maintain those components and key features that have worked.

In this second edition, you will see the following changes:

- More explicit explanation on how to select words to teach
- Addition of a Tier 2 words and phrases list as requested over the years
- Fine tuning of the preteaching vocabulary steps
- Addition of Step 7 as an accountability step

- Refined ideas for that critical Step 6
- Polished the Partner Reading + Summarization strategy
- Descriptions of Triad Reading + Summarization for Newcomers
- Elaboration on addressing state and language standards
- Close reading strategies for teaching ELs
- How to generate richer discussions and argumentative speech
- Two new chapters on writing and how it helps consolidate comprehension
- Revamped chapter on professional development strategies, coaching, administrator support, and whole-school endeavors

We retain our mission—to find appropriate ways to foster English Learners' reading skills that lead to academic success. For as we know, secondary level ELs are more likely to have experienced many challenges. Many need additional instruction due to interrupted schooling, while others have zero-English proficiency such as our EL Newcomers. All require substantial educational growth in a short amount of time. Secondary-school-age children present educators with unique and specific challenges for core content instruction, literacy, and language proficiency.

This updated book attempts to address some of these challenges by combining our experiences, continuous research, and practice as they emerge from the original set of longitudinal studies in various parts of the United States and other English-speaking territories/countries. The Carnegie Corporation of New York, the U.S. Department of Education's Institute for Education Sciences, and the U.S. Department of Education's Native Americans Projects funded these studies. Standardized language and reading and subject-matter measures, as well as formative assessments, were used to collect information on what strategies are successful in closing the achievement gap for English learners from different language backgrounds, learning in a variety of English structured immersion, sheltered English, and dual language programs.

Developing literacy skills for secondary school students is not easy. Secondary school literacy skills are more complex and more embedded in subject matters than in primary schools (Biancarosa & Snow, 2004). In their publication on adolescent literacy titled *Reading Next,* these two authors assert that subject matter literacy

- Includes reading, writing, and oral discourse for school
- Varies from subject to subject
- Requires knowledge of multiple genres of text, purposes for text use, and text media

- Is influenced by students' literacies in contexts outside of school
- Is influenced by students' personal, social, and cultural experiences

For ELs and struggling older readers, reading becomes an insurmountable task without explicit instruction on reading each of the subject matter texts. Fortunately, through ongoing studies specifically designed for adolescent EL literacy, educators now have a powerful array of tools at their disposal. We know from the data that these tools work well for non-EL striving readers. We initially spent 3 years "components testing" to find the best instructional and professional development combinations for addressing students' and teachers' needs. Subsequently, we have learned so much more from teachers and administrators who continue to implement the combinations. The combination of components, strategies, and performance assessment tools has been arranged in a framework that we call Expediting Comprehension for English Language Learners (ExC-ELL™).

Recommendations for Instructional Components

If we want students to read well—comprehend and learn the content—we must start integrating academic language with literacy in the content areas. We have identified 12 premises for this framework. Some components are aimed at helping teachers improve student achievement. Others are for helping teachers be successful themselves. These are the recommendations derived from the multiple ongoing studies thus far:

1. Teachers need assistance and models for developing lessons that integrate subject matter content, language, reading, and writing skills. There are five lesson-planning components that help teachers integrate these features into a cohesive lesson plan. Twelve instructional components are used to deliver the integrated instruction.

2. Teaching subject matter to ELs requires direct, explicit instruction in the strategies students need to build vocabulary and comprehend grade-level texts. The subject matter "Mentor Texts"— those that give explicit examples of the skills about to be learned—provide context and content that facilitate comprehension and success.

3. Students need to learn how to read a variety of texts that progress to grade-level texts quickly. To master content and meet standards, teachers learn how to parse texts and select most important content. Teachers select the district's content standards, objective, indicators ("I can" statements), purposes, outcomes, and targets, and scan the text once more for eliminating unnecessary information and highlighting information that addresses the standard.

4. Explicitly teaching depth and breadth of words found in the texts students will be reading, before, during, and after reading, is a primary role of all content teachers.

5. Collaborative text-based reading engages students with text, peer verbal summarization after each paragraph, and rich discussions where the new words are used repeatedly.

6. Explicitly teaching reading and writing skills is just as important in secondary as it is in elementary schools, notwithstanding adaptations in delivery:

   • Teachers select comprehension strategy (e.g., main idea, cause and effect, inferences, comparing/contrasting, self-correction, rereading a sentence, decoding a word, summarizing, questioning the author, questioning the information in the text, questioning ourselves.
   • Teachers conduct Read-Alouds to model fluency, close reading, and comprehension strategies.
   • Students conduct partner reading summarizing after each paragraph to practice comprehension strategies and comprehend content.
   • Teachers debrief with whole class about the content and the skills (linguistic, metalinguistic, comprehension, social, and cooperative learning) that they learned.

7. Explicitly teaching the different writing genre required by each content area, including the various formats for technology.

8. Consolidation of content and skills. Teachers use strategies throughout the lesson to anchor knowledge, check for understanding, and assess individual student learning.

9. Student assessments include a variety of formats to gauge learning progressions on language, literacy, and content.

10. The quality of implementation is assessed with specific observation protocols supported by expert and peer coaching to have instant

reports for teachers and administrators. Coaches and administrators need to be trained to observe this type of instruction.

11. Systematic and comprehensive professional development workshops and coaching throughout the year is necessary to sustain any program, approach, or instructional change.

12. Teacher Learning Communities for collegial efficacy help teachers with implementation hurdles and to learn from one another.

Organization of the Book

Since using only three or four of these components is unlikely to yield positive results for students or teachers, the chapters show how the topic is integrated, founded upon, or supports the other components.

Chapter 1. **"Introduction: The ExC-ELL Model for Content Knowledge, Literacy, and Academic Language Integration":** The introductory chapter details the background of the ExC-ELL study. It also states several "myths" that have been around for many years, such as "it takes 7 years to learn a language," which often hold back students and keep teachers from delivering challenging, rigorous, yet sensitive instruction to ELs. Each myth is followed by a "good news" section that dispels that myth and offers empirically tested recommendations instead.

Chapter 2. **"Planning Lessons Using a Research-Based Design":** This chapter gives a detailed background of the research for each of the ExC-ELL components. Each component was carefully selected based on the amount of reliable scientific research available. Each of the 12 lesson components was empirically tested across a variety of classrooms and with different language groups to gauge applicability and appropriateness. Refinements were made during the first 2 years of the study and are ongoing as we work with teachers throughout the country. With a new Title III 5-year grant from the U.S. Department of Education's Office of English Language Acquisition (OELA), we will be implementing ExC-ELL in more middle and high schools to train hundreds of teachers, administrators, and coaches to refine the model even further with accompanying data.

Chapter 3. **"Vocabulary Development: Selecting for High-Impact Usage and Comprehension":** This chapter goes further in-depth about vocabulary. The 2007 theoretical framework for selecting and teaching vocabulary to ELs was presented at the Pacific Regional

Educational Laboratory conference on Vocabulary: Research and Practice, where researchers such as Isabel Beck, Diane August, Freddie Hiebert, Michael Kamil, Steve Stahl, and others were kind enough to give us feedback. Once refined, we tested a few instructional strategies and then let the teachers run free with their own creative ways of teaching. Our 2017 version adds all the refinements from the past 10 years. In the ExC-ELL lesson delivery sequence, the teacher still begins with vocabulary instruction so students can comprehend and engage during reading, the processing and mastering of information, and text-based writing.

Chapter 4. **"Bridging Vocabulary and Reading"**: This chapter deals with the heart of the program—reading comprehension. While it presents comprehension strategies that work with ELs, it also emphasizes all the other instructional features that need to be in place for comprehension to work. It presents ideas for consolidating student knowledge after they have read a text. The consolidation of knowledge can take several forms, from instructional conversations with the teacher, students with students, to students formulating Bloom's Taxonomy-type questions, using Cooperative Learning strategies, graphic organizers in teams to writing strategies, and finally debriefing with students what they have learned. There needs to be a different approach to teaching reading in secondary schools. Therefore, a set of guiding questions is used to help teachers integrate reading into their existing lessons and content standards.

Chapter 5. **"Content Reading"**: This chapter highlights the challenges ELs and striving readers encounter daily and ways that content teachers can prepare their lessons to include simple basic reading strategies. Concomitantly, close reading strategies are gradually brought into the reading. The chapter specifies how science, math, social studies, electives, and language arts teachers can integrate those strategies for introducing text-based reading, while addressing the content objectives and standards for a lesson. Ways of getting 100% engagement in reading are detailed. The reading strategies enable all students to use new vocabulary, frequently summarize orally the contents using academic discourse, and going back into the text to find more key information. We discuss structures for Newcomers to participate in reading along with all other students to accelerate their learning.

Chapter 6. **"After Initial Reading"**: Once the students have read and summarized orally the contents of a selected text, there are other strategies that help anchor language, reading skills, and content learning. Students return to the text to formulate questions and answer peer questions, approaching these with higher-order thinking strategies. Exciting ways of engaging in close reading is one of the goals for after reading since we want the students to master the content they have been reading. Other strategies for consolidating knowledge, language, and literacy are presented such as a variety of Cooperative Learning and class debriefing techniques. Ideas for formative assessment of the whole reading process are offered, as well as the sequence for a lesson design.

Chapter 7. **"Writing Increases and Consolidates Vocabulary, Reading, and Content Learning":** Writing is the final proof that students have mastered new vocabulary and reading comprehension skills, when students can write about the content they are studying, using ideas, details, evidence from a text, and own opinions based on facts. There are popular writing programs that have been proven ineffective for ELs. We describe here the components of an effective writing approach that fits all content areas. This chapter offers evidence-based strategies for drafting, revising, and editing small and large pieces of writing. Specific rubrics for student self-assessment and ownership of editing and proofing are also discussed and modeled.

Chapter 8. **"Diving Deeper Into Writing":** There are several ways to integrate the revising and editing strategies into other types of writing. This chapter describes the types of writing for science, social studies, math, and language arts. It also adds more instructional supports for creative writing, critical thinking, selecting rubric criteria, and working with text structures and features in writing. Most important, it highlights the type of academic language students can use.

Chapter 9. **"Setting the Context for Success":** This chapter steers away from instruction and lesson design to a critical topic: professional development and continuous learning communities in schools. After a professional development session, be it a summer institute or within the school year, on comprehensive programs such as ExC-ELL, school administrators want to know what is the best follow-up and systematic support they can give their teachers, so all new learnings are implemented with quality and as much comfort as possible for the teacher. Strengthening collective teacher efficacy via Teacher Learning Communities leads to strengthening coaches' and site administrators' efficiency as well. Principals, supervisors, and coaches also need to be part of the training and work to support the implementation in the classroom. The collective efficacy becomes the change strategy in the school. This chapter offers ideas on sustaining the innovation through various support mechanisms. This chapter also provides tools for self-assessment and peer coaching using the ExC-ELL Observation Protocol. The Protocol can also be used by the teachers to observe their students, to plan their lessons, and to reflect on their practice.

Chapter 10. **"Implementing ExC-ELL: A Principal's Perspective":** This chapter provides insights from a middle school principal in Memphis, Tennessee, who has been trained in ExC-ELL and has invested in her staff and the students to train and coach the majority of her staff in ExC-ELL. She discusses the process for whole-school implementation, where her school is now and the next steps going forward. Also provided in her words are tools for school administrators, literacy coaches, content coaches, and district level professional development teams on how to observe, reflect, and coach teachers implementing ExC-ELL using a District Support Cadre model.

Acknowledgments

The first edition of this book was written with the help of Dr. Liliana Minaya-Rowe, Argelia Carreón, María N. Trejo, and Ashley Fitch. We are indebted to the teachers from Kapa'a Middle and Kapa'a High Schools, the Kawai District Office administrators, and resource specialists for their commitment to the testing of the original version. In New York City schools, we saw M. S. 319 in Washington Heights go from a reconstituted school to an exemplary school in 2 years. The principal, Ysidro Abreu, led his faculty to a quality implementation of ExC-ELL that enabled us to learn about the administrator's leadership role.

For this second edition, we are most indebted to our current team that helps us train teachers throughout the country and abroad: Dr. Maria N. Trejo, Dr. Hector Montenegro, Argelia Carreón, Elma Noyola, Elizabeth Montes, Guadalupe Espino, Joanne Marino, Carlos Ramírez, Karen Solis, Anita Crowley, Dr. Joy Peyton, Alexis Glick, and Barbara Cohen.

The vice president of Margarita Calderón & Associates, Inc. and coauthor, Shawn Slakk, has made many of the contributions that are reflected in this second edition.

As part of the learning process for the authors, we look at how we train, present, and coach the teachers we serve. At times, that service has taken on interesting variations. One interesting extension of ExC-ELL is in the form of Massachusetts' Rethinking Equity and Teaching for English Language Learners (RETELL) initiative. Beginning in June 2012, as a response to the need to provide equal educational opportunities for ELs in Massachusetts, the state's core academic educators (classroom and supervisory) are required by state law to earn a Sheltered English Immersion (SEI) endorsement. This ongoing endorsement process took more than 4 years to train more than 40,000 licensed educators: teachers and administrators. It involved developing several variations of a 45-hour graduate-level course based upon the components of ExC-ELL, training more than

250 RETELL instructors over the 4 years, developing a new teacher educator licensure test, and guiding the state's teacher preparation programs to infuse RETELL (a.k.a. ExC-ELL) strategies and techniques into their curricula as well. All at no cost to the educators themselves.

For transparency sake, the authors of this book were highly involved in the process. Margarita was selected by the U.S. Department of Justice, Civil Rights Division (DOJ), and the Department of Education, Office for Civil Rights (OCR), as their expert witness in the successful instruction of ELs. Shawn was hired as the RETELL Coordinator for the Massachusetts Department of Elementary and Secondary Education's Office of English Language Acquisition & Academic Achievement.

The implementation of ExC-ELL throughout the state of Virginia has helped advance the model considerably. We are most grateful to Virginia's ESL Professional Development Coordinator, Judy Radford, for sponsoring our institutes throughout the state and offering mini-grants to schools/districts to start ExC-ELL. We are most grateful to Loudoun County Public Schools for being the first to request a whole-school approach to professional development in a middle and high school. Based on their first-year results, two more secondary schools agreed to be part of the National Professional Development Title III grant from OELA. This next phase of implementation, data collection, and documentation will yield a stronger model to share with other schools.

We want to particularly thank Andrés Henríquez at the Carnegie Corporation of New York for his ideas, support, and the trust he placed in us to create and empirically study in experimental-control schools ExC-ELL for 4 years to make sure it had the evidence necessary to make it an effective model for all content teachers in secondary schools.

We would also like to thank Dr. Tarcia Gilliam-Parrish for her insight and contribution provided in Chapter 10 and to her staff for their hard work infusing ExC-ELL into their lessons and instruction.

Moreover, we couldn't have captured all about this effective model without the interest, support, and mentoring of our great friend Dan Alpert and most recent friend Maura Sullivan. The Corwin staff, Erin, Christine, Amy and Katie, are always ready to facilitate all preconference and conference logistics.

The contributions of the following reviewers for the first edition are gratefully acknowledged:

Mary Enright

National Board-Certified Teacher

New York State Education Department

Office of Bilingual Education
Albany, NY

Al Payne
Administrative Director
Regional Center IV
Miami-Dade County Public Schools
Miami, FL

Patricia Schwartz
Principal
Thomas Jefferson Middle School
Teaneck, NJ

Neal Glasgow
Teacher and Author
San Dieguito Academy
Encinitas, CA

Arlene Myslinski
EL Teacher
Buffalo Grove High School
Buffalo Grove, IL

David Bautista
Bilingual Director
Woodburn School District
Western University
Woodburn, OR

Nadia Mykysey
Adjunct Faculty at Temple University
Curriculum, Instruction and Technology in Education (CITE)
Philadelphia, PA

About the Authors

 **Margarita Espino Calderón,** a native of Juárez, Mexico, is Professor Emerita and Senior Research Scientist at Johns Hopkins University's Graduate School of Education. She is President/CEO of Margarita Calderón & Associates, Inc.

Margarita has served on several national panels, among others The National Research Council's Committee on Teacher Preparation; the U.S. Department of Education Institute for Education Sciences' National Literacy Panel for Language Minority Children and Youth; the Carnegie Adolescent English Language Learners Literacy Panel; and the California Pre-School Biliteracy Panel.

She was principal investigator in three 5-year studies on *Expediting Reading Comprehension for English Language Learners (ExC-ELL) Programs,* one that focuses on professional development of science, social studies, and language arts teachers in New York City's middle and high schools, funded by the Carnegie Corporation of New York; and two other studies, the Bilingual Cooperative Reading and Composition (BCIRC) in El Paso, Texas, and another funded by the U.S. Department of Education in the Pacific Islands for fourth- and fifth-grade teachers and students, and in middle and high schools in Alaska.

She was co-principal investigator with Robert Slavin on the 5-year national randomized evaluation of English immersion, transitional, and two-way bilingual programs, funded by the Institute for Education Sciences. She has published over 100 articles, chapters, books, and teacher training manuals and is invited to present at national and international conferences and professional development events.

Shawn Slakk is the VP of Operations and Senior Consultant/Master Coach for Margarita Calderón and Associates, Inc. He is coauthor and codeveloper of professional development sessions for all levels of educators, focusing on whole-school implementation, administrative support, and coaching. He is a former Certified WIDA Trainer and Title III SIOP Coach. He is the former Rethinking Equity and Teaching for English Language Learners (RETELL) Coordinator for the Massachusetts Department of Elementary and Secondary Education, the required endorsement for all teachers and administrators in the state. Shawn and his team developed, implemented, and evaluated the training of trainers for RETELL.

Shawn has taught ESL in grades K–University, Spanish, and even once taught Japanese to K–2 students. He has served as an elementary and middle school administrator, and District Office SIOP coach.

Shawn holds bachelor's degrees in English Education K–12 and Spanish Education K–12 from Whitworth College, a master's degree in Teaching English as a Second Language from Eastern Washington University, and a master's degree in School Administration from the University of North Carolina: Greensboro; he is completing his Ed.D. at the University of Virginia with a focus on reading instruction.

1

Introduction

The ExC-ELL Model for Content Knowledge, Literacy, and Academic Language Integration

"How can my ELs ever catch up?"

—Tenth-grade government teacher

Many middle and high school teachers and principals are asking us what to do about the large numbers of English Learners (ELs) coming to their schools. The way they have been teaching English as a Second Language (ESL) is not working. Trying to address all the Newcomers and the variety of proficiency levels of ELs across the grade levels overwhelms the lone ranger ESL/ELD teacher. Teachers can't find enough sheltered materials that cover the important facts and concepts, much less the district's standards. The seventh- and tenth-grade ELs are not passing the high-stakes tests. Teachers and principals are being held accountable for poor test scores, and both fear their jobs are on the line.

Organizations such as the Alliance for Excellent Education (www.a114ed.org), National Association of Secondary School Principals (www.nassp.org), and the Carnegie Corporation of New York (www.carnegie.org) have also been preoccupied with this issue. The Carnegie Corporation approached us in 2002 to develop a professional development (PD) program that could begin to address the needs of ELs and teachers in secondary schools.

Therefore, the project *Expediting Comprehension for English Language Learners* (ExC-ELL) was funded in 2003 for 5 years of testing by the Carnegie Corporation of New York to develop and study the effects of a PD model for *middle and high school teachers of English, science, mathematics, and social studies who work with ELs.* Recently, the basic components of ExC-ELL were the foundation for the Massachusetts PD initiative called RETELL (Rethinking Equity and Teaching for English Language Learners). RETELL has become part of Massachusetts' licensure requirements to renew, advance, or earn a teaching license in the commonwealth of Massachusetts. The purpose of this book is to share the PD and instructional components developed and tested in sixth- to twelfth-grade classrooms. The information and strategies outlined in subsequent chapters were tested from New York City to Hawaii in classrooms with multiple language student backgrounds.

Why the Model Worked

Since most ELs are in heterogeneous classrooms that include English-only students (in the five pilot schools, the number ranged from 10% to 90% ELs in each classroom), the staff development program was designed to help teachers provide effective instruction *for ELs and all other students in their classrooms, particularly those reading below grade level and needing extensive vocabulary development.* Student data indicated significant results not just for ELs, but also for all students in the participating classrooms. Teachers reported these same strategies were particularly helpful with African American and Hawaiian students who needed additional work with vocabulary and reading skills. The PD and instructional components are described in chapters throughout this book.

In addition to the teacher training program, PD sessions were designed for *literacy coaches, content curriculum specialists, principals, and central office administrators* on how to observe and coach teachers as they deliver their lessons integrating reading, writing, and vocabulary development along with their content. The ExC-ELL Observation Protocol called the WISEcard (Walkthroughs for Instructional Strategies via ExC-ELL) was developed and tested for validity and reliability by teams consisting of a principal, associate superintendent, coach, university professor, and teachers.

The ExC-ELL Observation Protocol WISEcard is also used as a classroom tool for

- Planning content lessons
- Coaching by literacy coaches not familiar with EL instruction
- Coaching or supervision by administrators
- Teacher self-reflection
- Peer and Teacher Learning Community (TLC) coaching and modeling
- Conducting classroom research

A second 5-year study will be training whole-school staffs from several school districts, known as school divisions, in Virginia and studying the features of implementation and impact on students and teachers. This study is in collaboration with George Washington University and funded by the U.S. Department of Education's Office of English Language Acquisition.

Benefits for Schools, Principals, Teachers, and Students

First No Child Left Behind, and now ESSA (Every Student Succeeds Act), calls for reform and accountability for ELs and all students reading below grade level. Secondary schools need to improve and need help toward that goal. If schools want to improve student performance, it means they must begin by improving the performance of all teachers, particularly teachers in middle and high schools who have *ELs and other adolescents reading below grade level.*

Limited English language skills and low academic performance of Hispanic and other language-minority students pose a major problem in the middle and high school settings. Middle school and high school language-minority students must be ready to participate in a rigorous academic program, and the time for this preparation is limited, which often allows ELs only superficial learning of vocabulary and concepts. Consequently, they are never up to par with the literacy levels and academics demanded by secondary school curricula. Subsequently, most middle and high school language-minority students fail to develop to their fullest potential. As a result, they become disaffected, drop out of school, and many settle for low-paying jobs or no jobs at all because they have little or no access to either high school or a college education (RAND, 2002; Slavin & Calderón, 2001).

Most teachers do not receive adequate preparation to teach the language-minority students before entering the workforce and have limited opportunities to update their knowledge and skills in an ongoing basis throughout their careers (Calderón & Minaya-Rowe, 2003). Teachers' lack of preparedness is a serious problem because the opportunities for at-risk students to succeed academically depend on teachers' knowledge and application of effective teaching in the classroom. According to the U.S. Department of Education, 42% of public school teachers have at least one EL in the classroom, only 27% of teachers of ELs feel highly qualified to teach them, and only 30% of teachers of ELs have received PD in teaching these students (Leos, 2006). The Learning First Alliance (2000) reports teachers in general may be educated, licensed, and employed without knowledge of the most important tools for fighting illiteracy. Seventeen years later, this issue persists. School districts are still struggling to find qualified teachers.

To equip all teachers to work successfully with a growing at-risk population requires continuing renewal and extension of the skills, knowledge, and awareness needed to remain effective in a multi-cultural dynamic environment (Darling-Hammond & Sykes, 2003). ESSA calls for professional qualifications of teachers and profound knowledge of

- Student academic achievement disaggregated by subgroups
- Comparison of students at basic, proficient, and advanced levels of language and literacy development
- Assessment processes, interpretation of data, and implications for instructional improvement
- An ample instructional repertoire that reaches all students

New and experienced teachers need the type of PD that allows them to explore their beliefs about their students and increase their repertoire of linguistic and culturally relevant pedagogy (Calderón, 2000; Calderón, Carreón, Slakk, & Peyton, 2017). This also places teachers' needs within a larger context that includes institutional missions and goals, student performance data, and teacher support mechanisms. An institution's

> Teachers cannot possibly be fully prepared without quality preservice and quality ongoing PD. Results-driven education and quality teaching require teacher-focused quality PD.

program (school district or university) must include measures for student performance and for measuring changes in educators' on-the-job performance. But it must also apply those same measures to the institution preparing the teachers.

For instance, by July 2016, to renew, advance, or retain their educator license, Massachusetts required its 40,000 teachers plus the 15,000 administrators who supervise these teachers to earn the RETELL Endorsement by participating in a state-created graduate level course designed to meet the needs of ELs. Not only did it require current educators to earn this endorsement, but it also required the state's teacher preparation institutions to update their syllabi to reflect the ExC-ELL based strategies contained in the RETELL instruction courses.

One area that needs dire attention and quality comprehensive PD programs is *reading*. Although everyone in the nation is preoccupied with developing reading skills for all students, including ELs, scarce attention is given to effective designs of professional programs to develop the teachers' skills for *teaching reading within the context of rigorous content instruction.*

As schools continuously shift from one reading program to another, when balanced literacy becomes unbalanced, and schools look for another reading text or program, the best recourse is to prepare all teachers to incorporate evidence-based reading strategies into all their daily instructional components.

Myths From the Past Still Haunt Us!—But There's Good News!

Although there continues to be a high interest in ELs at secondary schools since the *Reading Next* report (Department of Education's focus on adolescent literacy), there have been prevalent beliefs, practices, and policies that have prevented the implementation of quality instructional programs for ELs. Some misconceptions have been the following:

- The belief that it takes 5 to 7 years to become proficient in English
- The misconception that ESL/ELD or sheltered instruction teachers can meet all the needs of each EL student by themselves, and mainstream content teachers do not have to and cannot teach ELs

- The focus of instruction in ESL/ELD classrooms should only be oral language development.
- Special classes need to be set up where content and English are simplified to the point that they are watered down to make them comprehensible for ELs.
- All ELs need the same type of ESL/ELD program, same phonics-based interventions, and to be placed in the same classroom together.

Yes, *it used to* take 5 to 7 years. It may still take that long when ELs are placed in elementary schools where the transition from primary language into English instruction is delayed until the fourth, fifth, or sixth grade or when English language instruction is left only to the ESL/ELD teacher. By then, it is too late for students to catch up and be fully prepared for middle school and beyond. It may also take 5 to 7 years when the pacing of instruction is too relaxed and not challenging enough. After spending 5 to 7 years learning only or mainly in their primary language, students become accustomed and do not feel the need to learn English, since they've gotten along without it for so long.

As they go up the grade levels, the difficulty of the dense textbooks they encounter also goes up. This becomes a greater and greater challenge when students are not used to rigorous (but relevant and explicit) instruction in English. Unless ELs learn 3,000 to 5,000 words in English from K to twelfth grade, they will never catch up with their mainstream peers. By the time they graduate from high school, they should own at least 50,000 words in their verbal repertoire to be college or career ready (Graves, August, & Carlo, 2011). If all teachers—core content, ESL, special education teachers, and specialist—are not teaching vocabulary daily, the students will not be able to keep up with their academic challenges. Chapter 3 details how to accomplish this.

At the other extreme, instruction in the early grades might have been paced so fast students could never catch up! This fast-track pacing leaves huge gaps in the normal development of basic skills such as grammar, spelling, composition, and most important, reading comprehension. If these students are then transitioned into all-English instruction in the first or second grade, they may never catch up.

In secondary schools, Newcomers, Students with Interrupted Formal Education (SIFE), and Long-Term ELs (LT-ELs) are usually clustered together in the same ESL/ELD classroom. Moreover, they are either immersed immediately into difficult content courses with pull-out or push-in ESL/ELD support (which has no evidence of being effective), or they take ESL and sheltered content classes that may not be rigorous enough to meet state standards. What we want schools to espouse is the *balancing act between rigor, relevancy, and sensitivity* so that all teachers of ELs integrate language and reading in their active teaching repertoires.

Good News

Through several randomized scientific studies, we are seeing how instruction can be carefully designed to accelerate the learning rate of literacy in English at whatever grade level ELs enter. These studies also show instruction can facilitate the learning of two languages simultaneously. For instance, students can learn to speak, read, and write in English and Spanish in two-way bilingual programs (TWB). In two-way/dual-language bilingual programs, mainstream and language minority students become bilingual and biliterate when instructed in both languages from prekindergarten on—just as many people in other countries have done for centuries. Well-designed dual-language programs for middle and high schools are now functioning effectively in sites such as El Paso, Texas, and New York City.

> MYTH: It takes 5 to 7 years to become proficient in English. **DEBUNKED!**

Testing requirements for secondary schools are having detrimental effects on ELs. The Hispanic dropout rate is at its highest in history. English language learners are not making adequate yearly progress. Those students who make it to universities face a 75% chance they will fail and drop out the first year. If school administrators want their ELs to show annual yearly progress, to pass state assessments, and to succeed in life, then they must hire well-prepared teachers or prepare them themselves through comprehensive inservice programs, with the latter being the most viable option.

Every state in the nation will attest to the fact that there is a critical shortage of bilingual and ESL/ELD credentialed teachers, particularly secondary teachers. However, this does not preclude offering PD for all teachers in the school who are working with or soon will be working with a handful or many ELs in their classrooms as Massachusetts has done. In fact, providing PD should be a requirement. Highly qualified teachers in core subjects, including Language Arts or English as a Second Language should be the norm. Some states require all educators (teachers and administrators) to have some coursework on working with EL populations, but teachers report it is rarely sufficient to address their students' needs, particularly when it comes to EL reading difficulties.

Good News

Some schools, districts, and state departments of education have already taken steps toward and beyond ESSA or whatever other requirements come around by offering comprehensive PD programs for *all* their teachers. State departments of education, such as Washington state, began training all educators on EL issues in 2005. New York City schools began retraining hundreds of teachers on current research-based literacy in Spanish. They offered schools $20,000 to begin planning ways of restructuring their programs to better address the needs of ELs and to establish more two-way bilingual schools. They also offered that amount for language, literacy, and content programs such as RIGOR (Reading Instructional Goals for Older Readers) to train teachers and provide daily lessons (Calderón, 2007). The island of Kauai began setting the pace for other islands in the state of Hawaii. They accomplished this by establishing, at the district level, learning communities where the superintendent and his education specialists worked collaboratively to learn and create ways of supporting learning for all educators in the district with a strong focus on EL literacy.

> MYTH: ESL/ELD or sheltered instruction teachers can meet all the needs of each EL student by themselves and mainstream content teachers do not have to and cannot teach ELs. **DEBUNKED!**

In most secondary schools, there appears to be a chasm between the ESL/ELD and the content classrooms. The ESL/ELD teacher is supposed to concentrate on "getting those kids to speak English" and the content teachers to impart content. For decades, ESL meant learning basic words in English, enough to help students express themselves and understand basic instructions from teachers in mainstream classrooms. This very basic vocabulary is what we call Tier 1 words. They are important for building Tier 2- and 3-word knowledge germane to conceptual understanding of the sciences, social studies, and math coursework (for a broader definition and examples of Tier 1–3 words, please see Chapter 3). However, a whole semester or more is too long in a student's scholastic life to spend on Tier 1 words. For example, we recently observed a high school ESL/ELD teacher who spent 50 minutes teaching 10 words about professions (e.g., carpenter, engineer, teacher). The teacher used props, pictures, and gestures to present each word. After providing information on each, he asked his eight students to work in pairs to match the words with a definition he provided in an envelope. He walked around and helped the students who needed help. The students mostly worked silently, moving the pieces around, until the teacher gave them a thumbs up. Before the period ended, we decided to give the students a test on the 10 words. The most they remembered were five words. In other words, 50 minutes were spent "teaching" but not "reaching." This instructional event reinforces how ESL/ELD teachers may be doing a lot of work, well intended, but not in the most efficient and effective manner.

Good News

In the past 10 years, research that focuses on vocabulary development for mainstream and ELs has shown promising practices for accelerating the learning of vocabulary in both ESL/ELD and mainstream classrooms. Although it is important to teach oral language, it cannot be separate from reading and writing development. In fact, exposure to the written word and basic reading skills helps students develop a larger vocabulary. Student mastery of a word means they can decode, pronounce, spell, define it, write a meaningful sentence with it, and recognize it in a different context. Ways of expediting mastery of words are described in the vocabulary chapter (Chapter 3).

MYTH: The focus of instruction in the English as a Second Language (ESL) classroom should be oral language development. **DEBUNKED!**

The term *sheltered classes* or *ESL/ELD content classes* are sometimes misconstrued as places where subject matter is adapted and/or watered down to very simplistic oral phrases and superficial concepts. Sheltered instruction calls for the teacher to use "appropriate speech" (Echevarria, Vogt, & Short, 2000), which at times turns out to be taught in a way that limits the growth of vocabulary. We observed a teacher who was so careful to select words her students would understand that she limited her vocabulary all semester long as well as the students' breadth and depth of word knowledge.

Students' linguistic and academic development is enormously hindered when they are submitted to semesters of this type of limited instruction. In cases like this, sheltered instruction focuses to the extreme on making content comprehensible. When it takes too much time for the teacher to show pictures, realia, make gestures, it leaves little time for students to interact with the new words and take ownership. Ownership occurs when a learner uses the new words in a contextual meaning. Although sheltered classes are intended to make rigorous content comprehensible, ESL(ELD)/sheltered content teachers need to monitor the extent of sheltering and the benefits students are deriving. Newcomer Centers often experience the same preoccupation with the balance of rigor and watered-down curricula and instructional strategies.

Good News

Academic language proficiency is the ability to make complex meanings explicit using appropriate language for that specific content area. It's not communicating through paralinguistic cues or choppy phrases. Academic language proficiency is the ability to read, discuss, and write about complex topics learned in school. All teachers—ESL/ELD, sheltered instruction, mainstream—can now be well equipped with ways to help students attain academic language proficiency.

MYTH: Special classes need to be set up where content and English are sheltered to make them comprehensible for ELs. **DEBUNKED!**

English Learners come to secondary schools with a wide range of linguistic, academic, and life skills. Typically, schools offer only one type of ESL/ELD course per grade level, where the whole range of students are placed. This makes it very difficult for the ESL/ELD teacher to address the array of needs. This teacher will most likely try to teach to the middle, limiting quality attention and instruction to the students in the higher and lower ends of the continuum.

The term *differentiated instruction* has come to mean a mainstream teacher can have a wide range of students in the same class and can use certain strategies to cope with this diversity. No matter how skilled a teacher is or how many workshops on differentiated instruction he or she has attended, the teacher may not adequately address literacy and oracy development.

In some cases, many ELs' problems stem not from lack of oral language development, but from a diversity of reading development difficulties. Long-Term ELs can express themselves in English quite well. These students may or may not be identified as Limited English Proficient (LEP) but have great difficulty comprehending texts in English. They have been poorly schooled and will need some basic phonics, along with phonemic and phonological awareness strategies through immediate interventions or in the context of reading. However, studies indicate after 20 or so lessons on phonics only, the effect diminished considerably (Kamil, 2005). Therefore, *semester-long phonics programs/instruction without focusing on other skills does not work for ELs.*

MYTH: All ELs need the same type of ESL/ELD program, same phonics-based interventions, and to be placed in the same classroom together. **DEBUNKED!**

In contrast, highly educated Newcomer ELs who are so well schooled and literate would feel insulted attending such phonics/phonemic awareness interventions. The intervention they need is ample vocabulary development and acquaintance with the basic protocols of classroom norms, social norms, an understanding of their teachers' expectations, and the variety of concepts of print for all the textbooks they will be using.

Good News

When schools are sensitive to their students, they find ways of assessing each student to find out what type of intervention is necessary—decoding, contrastive linguistics, fluency in speaking, fluency in reading, reading comprehension, spelling, writing mechanics, composition, more vocabulary development, grammar, etc. The amount of time for the intervention also varies. Some students may need a whole semester of reading instruction, while others only one-on-one tutoring for 2 or 3 weeks. Expediting reading comprehension entails providing the right type of instructional intervention as expeditiously as possible. This means Reading Specialists must be well trained to have an extensive repertoire of reading strategies and techniques and effective ways to teach vocabulary as a precursor into reading comprehension. They must also have appropriate materials to cover the range of necessary interventions. The interventions can take place after school, on Saturdays, or as electives. It is important to begin interventions as soon as possible at the beginning of the semester and to end the intervention when it is no longer necessary.

Summary

- ✓ There are many prevalent myths about EL instruction that keep teachers and students from reaching full potential.

- ✓ ELs benefit from carefully crafted and challenging content instruction.

- ✓ Teaching reading comprehension in the content areas can be achieved by combining components that have been empirically tested in classrooms with ELs.

- ✓ Successful teachers are supported by caring and knowledgeable coaches and administrators, school districts, and state departments of education such as Virginia's DOE who also know how language, reading, and content go together.

2

Planning Lessons Using a Research-Based Design

The literacy constructs described in Chapter 4 were incorporated into a 12-component instructional template that mainstream and ESL/ELD teachers piloted and continue to refine in the various iterations of ExC-ELL (Expediting Comprehension for English Language Learners) in different parts of the country. It was based on research and practice on second-language acquisition, reading comprehension, and writing skills development. Chapter 9 describes the parallel research on teacher efficacy, collective efficacy, and the professional development (PD) design.

Second-Language Learning

The strategies and programs in secondary schools that include reading comprehension strategies have been effective for the most part with mainstream students. A few programs have been widely tested with EL populations, but mainly with one or two subject matter areas. To our knowledge, none have been tested with ELs in middle and high school science, social studies, and language arts classrooms at the same schools. Recent studies have shown little or no effect and, in one case, negative effect on EL academic learning (August & Shanahan, 2006). The first edition of this book integrated second-language learning strategies within each of the 12 components based on the research findings at that time (August & Hakuta, 1997; Bialystok & Hakuta, 1994); and theoretical frameworks by Cummins (1984) and Krashen (1981, 1982). Since then, we added refined knowledge from the 2-year panel work on EL literacy by The National Literacy Panel on Language Minority Children and Youth (August & Shanahan, 2006) and the Carnegie Panel on literacy on adolescent ELs (Short & Fitzsimmons, 2007). Dr. Calderón was a member of both panels.

Sheltered English Instruction

The original ExC-ELL project used basic principles from Sheltered English Instruction (SEI) to develop the second-language needs of ELs (King, Fagan, Bratt, & Baer, 1987; Chamot & O'Malley, 1994; Echevarria, Vogt, & Short, 2000). The key components of SEI are lesson preparation, comprehensibility, lesson delivery, and interaction. SEI is scaffolded and mediated to provide refuge from the linguistic demands of English as a second-language (L2) discourse, which is beyond the current level of comprehension of the students. The theoretical underpinning of SEI is language acquisition enhanced through meaningful use of interaction. SEI can be described as a melding of elements of language acquisition principles and elements of quality teaching (Echevarria & Graves, 1998). Sociocultural theory also influences it because it occurs within social and cultural contexts. This approach facilitates a high level of student involvement and interaction in the classroom. Teachers present material in patterns related to their students' language and culture as well as that of the school. Through this approach, students learn new material through the lens of their own language and culture (Valdéz, 1996). One major caveat to consider about sheltered instruction is the lack of focus on reading and text-based writing. Moreover, teachers tend to shelter students too much or use watered-down lessons that hold back the mastery of vocabulary that is pivotal to learning content. This is most likely the reason 75% of ELs are Long-Term ELs.

Structured English Immersion

Another interpretation of SEI is called Structured English Immersion (Slavin & Cheung, 2004). This version of SEI includes basic reading and reading comprehension instruction followed by text-based writing, and it has shown better results than the sheltered English version.

Bilingual Education

The ExC-ELL project also evolved from the work generated by longitudinal studies conducted by Dr. Calderón and colleagues:

- OERI/IES 5-year study "Effective Programs for EL Literacy: The Bilingual Cooperative Integrated Reading and Composition (BCIRC) model of teaching in Spanish and English (Calderón, Hertz-Lazarowitz, & Slavin 1998). This was the precursor to the ExC-ELL study funded by the Carnegie Corporation of New York.
- Five-year "Randomized Study of Structured English Immersion, Transitional Bilingual, and Two-Way Bilingual Programs (90–10; 70–30; 50–50)"—Johns Hopkins University's Center for Data-Driven Reform in Education (2003–2008 and Calderón & Carreón, 1994).
- DELSS (NICHD/IES) 5-year study "Inter-linguistic, Intra-linguistic, and Developmental Factors of ELL Reading in Spanish and English"—A joint study by researchers from Johns Hopkins, Center for Applied Linguistics, Harvard, and Miami University reports (August, Calderón, & Carlo, 2001, 2002; August, Carlo, Calderon, & Proctor, 2005).
- IES 5-year randomized study "National Center for Data-Driven Reform in Education–The ELL Achievement Component"—Johns Hopkins University (Slavin, Madden, Calderón, Chamberlain, & Hennessy, 2009).

Based on the results from these studies, Calderón, Slavin, and Sánchez (2011) assert that the quality of instruction is what matters most in educating English learners. Concomitantly, the studies highlight comprehensive reform models, as well as individual components of the models: school structures and leadership; language and literacy instruction; integration of language, literacy, and content instruction in secondary schools; cooperative learning; professional development; parent and family support teams; tutoring; and monitoring implementation and outcomes. The collective components imply that a comprehensive whole-school approach to ELs' academic achievement is the best model for schools to implement.

As larger numbers of English learners reach America's schools, K–12 general education teachers are discovering the need to learn how to teach these students. Schools realize that the improvement of the skills of all educators through comprehensive PD is an ambitious, but necessary undertaking (Calderón et al., 2011).

The focus of the research and development proposed in this book is on translating the findings of explicit strategy instruction into practical, replicable techniques to make strategy instruction effective as a routine part of reading comprehension and English language development in science, social studies, math, and language arts classrooms with small or large numbers of ELs.

The ExC-ELL 12-Step Lesson Framework

Each component of the lesson has been based on research. A synthesis of this evidence-based research is included here so teachers and administrators can continue to pursue related research, conduct more profound studies, or use this information to write proposals that can fund their staff development programs or empirical studies of what works in their schools. The primary purpose, however, is to guide teachers through the development of their lessons once they have gone through the training and studied the background of each component.

Vocabulary Strategies

Word knowledge correlates with comprehension (Beck, McKeown, & Kucan, 2002; Cunningham & Stanovich, 1998; Juel, 1988; Nagy & Anderson, 1984; Samuels, 2002). For older struggling readers, the vocabulary in the books they read affects whether and how they achieve fluency and comprehension (Menon & Hiebert, 2003; Torgesen, Rashotte, Alexander, Alexander, & McFee, 2002). In other words, the size of a student's vocabulary bank predicts his or her level of reading comprehension. We frequently discuss with teachers when we work with them on this in their PD sessions, that yes, knowledge is power, but vocabulary denotes status. In today's terms, this means that the number of words known also predicts how ELs perform on high-stakes tests that call for any type of reading comprehension. Unless students know 85% to 95% of the words they are reading, comprehension will be stifled (Samuels, 2002). Vocabulary development strategies are of importance for all students, but especially for English Learners (Fitzgerald, 1995; García, 2000; Blachowicz & Fisher, 2000). Particularly promising vocabulary strategies include those described by Beck et al. (2002), Calderón et al. (2005), Calderón & Minaya-Rowe (2003), and Padrón (1992). August et al. (2002) propose the use of cognates (taught with derivational and inflectional morphemes and other strategies) as effective vocabulary tools for Spanish-speaking

ELs. This is particularly important in schools where 95% to 98% of the students in middle and high schools are Hispanic. All teachers need to explicitly teach vocabulary before, during, and after reading for purposes of ensuring comprehension.

————————O————————

Lesson Components Template

1. Preteaching of Vocabulary
2. Teacher Think-Alouds
3. Student Peer Reading
4. Peer Summaries
5. Depth of Word Studies/Grammar
6. Class Debriefings/Discussions
7. Cooperative Learning Strategies
8. Formulating Questions and Numbered Heads
9. Round Table Reviews
10. Pre-writing and Drafting
11. Revising/Editing
12. Reading Final Product

See our website www.ExC-ELL.com for the ExC-ELL Lesson Integration Tool template.

————————O————————

Activating Prior Knowledge

A common practice in ESL/ELD or SEI classrooms has been to do background building at the beginning of a lesson. Instead of helping, strategies such as the following hinder the learning of vocabulary and the development of reading comprehension: (1) Providing a summary of what students are about to read that gives away too much information and steers students away from wanting to read the text. The result is that many then feel that there is no reason to read it since they have just been told what it says. (2) Providing a translated summary or complete version of the text that prevents students from challenging themselves to read and learn the new language. Again, why bother when they already know what it contains. Also, it may not be beneficial if the student isn't literate in their primary language. (3) Spending too much of the precious 30 to 45 minutes some teachers have to deliver a whole lesson. Rather, instead of doing these time-consuming strategies, teachers can do a Think-Aloud using text-features or preteach necessary vocabulary, or clarify lesson objectives and expected outcomes. Finally, activating prior knowledge only works for those students who have sufficient connects to the lesson about to be presented.

Think-Alouds

Teachers' use of Think-Alouds is intended to help students examine and develop reading behaviors and strategies (Flower & Hayes, 1980; Olshavsky, 1976–1977). As teachers describe their own thoughts about a text, students realize how and when to do the same. Think-Alouds are a metacognitive verbalization of what is being read. As adults, we automatically do this silently as we read. It is, however, a skill that should be explicitly taught and therefore is used by ExC-ELL teachers for making predictions or showing how to develop hypotheses, describing one's visual images, sharing an analogy, or showing how prior knowledge applies, verbalizing a confusing point or show how to monitor developing understandings, and demonstrating fix-up strategies.

Fluency

Reading automaticity means decoding words with minimal attention to decoding and meaning of the words. Adult readers simply recognize the words instantly and accurately on sight. This type of processing frees the reader's conscious attention to comprehend or construct meaning from the text (Rasinski, 2000; Samuels, 2002). Not so for ELs if they are not able to recognize the words. Word knowledge must also be accompanied by prosody. Prosody stresses the appropriate use of phrasing and expression (Dowhower, 1987). When readers embed appropriate volume, tone, emphasis, phrasing, and other elements in oral expression, they are giving evidence of actively interpreting or constructing meaning from the passage—all of which must be modeled and taught for effective comprehension (Rasinski, 2000). ExC-ELL teachers read aloud the beginning segment of a text to model reading fluency for students. Students then reread that segment aloud with their partners and continue to read the remainder of the text with the partner, keeping in mind the strategies modeled by the teacher. Partner Read-Aloud provides teachers opportunities to walk around and monitor and record the progress of the ELs fluency. *(Please see WISEcard EOP® fluency checklist attached to the observation/ coaching protocol in Chapter 9.)*

Partner Reading

In Partner Reading, paired students take turns reading aloud to each other. Various forms of partnered reading have been found to produce significant gains in fluency and comprehension (Eldredge, 1990; Koskinen & Blum, 1986; Osborn, Lehr, & Hiebert, 2003; Slavin & Madden, 2001). The partner provides support as needed with new words and reading fluency. Partnered reading (1) provides students with many opportunities to practice reading, and (2) it provides students with guidance to how fluent readers read and with feedback to help them become aware of and correct their mistakes (Foorman & Mehta, 2002; Shanahan, 2002). Partner reading has been particularly effective with English Learners (Calderón et al., 1998; Stevens, Slavin, & Farnish, 1991), and both ELs and Spanish as a Second Language learners in two-way bilingual programs (Calderón & Minaya-Rowe, 2003). In the ExC-ELL program, teachers train students to use specific techniques paired with summarization or, alternatively, comprehension strategies for giving corrective feedback to each other. As a follow-up strategy to encourage close reading, students formulate their own study questions and answers or look for story grammar elements, critical events, or scientific process steps.

Summarization

Having students summarize information they have read is one of the most consistently supported of all cognitive reading comprehension and study strategies (Brown & Day, 1983; Palincsar & Brown, 1984; Padrón & Waxman, 1988; Rosenshine & Meister, 1994; Slavin & Madden, 2001; Taylor & Beach, 1984). Armbruster, Anderson, and Ostertag (1987) successfully evaluated a particular form of summarization that analyzed social studies content into three boxes: statement of a problem, actions taken to solve the problem, and results of the actions.

Malone and Mastropieri (1992) found summarization was made more effective if students with reading disabilities were also taught to monitor their own summaries using a checklist. One of the ExC-ELL strategies is for students to alternate sentences to read a paragraph with a partner, and then together orally summarize what was read. Another partner reading strategy is to read a paragraph and then formulate a test question that gets at the essence of that paragraph. At times, partners simply state, "This is what we found" in the paragraph; then, they summarize what they found in the complete page. Breaking up text into smaller chunks such as paragraphs enables ELs to process information more profoundly and recall it. ELs also learn to parse the text and analyze it carefully for details and main points with a peer. This helps them to do the same type of analysis during test taking.

Story Grammar/Text Formats

Another form of facilitated summarization that has been successfully evaluated is having students identify story grammar in narratives. That is, students identify the main characters, setting, problem, attempted problem solutions, and final solutions. Short and Ryan (1984) found this strategy to help students understand text. Idol (1987) and Idol and Croll (1987) had upper-elementary children use a "story map" that focused on the same story grammar elements, and this helped poor readers to comprehend the content. Pointing out characteristics of formats used by math, science, and social studies texts helps ELs understand the focus of the lesson. ExC-ELL uses story maps and a variety of cognitive and semantic maps to help students comprehend and retain content.

Text-Based Question Generation

Another robust strategy for comprehension and vocabulary development is teaching young adolescents to generate their own questions about the material they are reading. For example, Davey and McBride (1986) taught sixth graders to develop "think-type" questions as they read. This strategy helped students understand and recall the key ideas. King (1994) successfully used a similar strategy, and question generation is a central feature of reciprocal teaching. A variant focused on vocabulary development is "Questioning the Author" (Beck & McKeown, 1991), in which students are taught a strategy for expository text in which they ask why an author included certain information or explanations. Charts with key verbs and question starters are used by ExC-ELL teachers to help students formulate higher-level questions of different types (e.g., remember, understand, apply, analyze, evaluate, create). Key to this process is also writing the answer to the question. Finally, cooperative learning is involved as these questions are turned into whole-class discussions and reviews.

Interaction and Transactional Strategies Instruction

The term *transactional strategies instruction* is used by Pressley and Woloshyn (1995) to refer to a set of related programs that were designed to teach a variety of reading comprehension strategies. The specific strategies emphasized include prediction, reacting to text, constructing images to represent ideas, checking back in the text, generating questions, and summarizing.

The term *coaching* has also been applied to these types of interaction events (Taylor, Pearson, Peterson, & Rodriguez, 2003). Instructional Conversations (Saunders, 2001; Saunders & Goldenberg, 1999) is another variation. Instructional Conversations (ICs) emphasize culturally responsive instruction where teachers help ELs with language and knowledge-based differences as they interpret content presented in textbooks. The ExC-ELL process uses the ICs to engage students with other students in the learning process by promoting rich language and academic involvement. Teachers model this via Think-Alouds and monitor student understanding, while students do their own Think-Alouds. The IC helps ELs develop thinking and problem-solving skills, as well as with forming, expressing and exchanging ideas in speech and in writing (Saunders & Goldenberg, 1999). The enacted IC promotes learning by weaving together prior knowledge, experiences, and new concepts (Tharp & Yamauchi, 1994). For ExC-ELL, we use the following indicators:

- Classroom management
- Clear academic goal
- Higher rate of student talk
- Students' views and ideas
- Students' preferences
- Levels of understanding
- Questioning and restating

The instructional elements in the IC enable the teacher to build background knowledge, while eliciting students' contributions and reasoning, and provide direct teaching when necessary in small teams or during a one-on-one consultation. The conversational elements of the IC promote teacher responsiveness to students and less "known-answer" questions that allow for interactive discourse and general participation in a challenging but non-threatening environment. These elements promote those higher Bloom's Taxonomy cognitive abilities, such as analysis, reflection, and critical thinking (Goldenberg, 1992/1993).

Reciprocal Teaching

Reciprocal Teaching is a reading technique which is thought to promote students' reading comprehension. A reciprocal approach provides students with four specific reading strategies that are actively and consciously used to support comprehension: Questioning, Clarifying, Summarizing, and Predicting (Palincsar, 1986). Reciprocal Teaching begins with the students and teacher reading a short piece of text together. Initially, the teacher models the four strategies required by Reciprocal Teaching, and teacher and students share in conversation about the text. The teacher then explicitly models his or her thinking processes out loud, using each of the four reading strategies. Students follow the teacher's model with their own strategies, also verbalizing their thought processes for the other students to hear.

After modeling, students are then ready to work in teams to reciprocally teach each other. Supports such as Table Tents or other guides with the roles for each teaching "job" helps all students, but is especially crucial for ELs. Additionally, crucial is sentence or summarizing starters that parallel the teaching role each student takes.

The Combination of Reading Strategies and Cooperative Learning

A variety of cooperative learning methods have been used to develop students' comprehension skills. For example, Dansereau (1988) have studied "cooperative scripts," in which students take turns summarizing and evaluating each other's summaries. Meloth and Deering (1992, 1994) found peers could help each other acquire cognitive strategies. Fantuzzo, Polite, and Grayson (1990) developed and evaluated reciprocal peer tutoring strategies to help students study complex material. Reciprocal Teaching is a method in which students work in cooperative learning groups to learn to make predictions, to generate questions about the text, to seek clarification when they did not understand, and to use summarization strategies (Palincsar & Brown, 1984). Cooperative Strategic Reading (Klingner & Vaughn, 1998) uses cooperative learning to teach skills such as previewing a text, brainstorming, predicting, identifying the most important information in a text, and then wrapping up what they have learned. Another study on Reciprocal Teaching was conducted specifically with ELs in which the teacher and students engaged in dialogue as students were instructed in four specific comprehension monitoring strategies: (a) summarizing, (b) self-questioning, (c) clarifying, and (d) predicting (Padrón, 1992). She found these reciprocal teaching strategies could be successfully taught to ELs when the teacher reads the text aloud to the students. When the teacher reads aloud, the teacher reading aloud helps ELs learn the four comprehension strategies without having to wait until they learn to decode. In ExC-ELL, the teacher reads only a small paragraph and does a Think-Aloud to model comprehension strategies. The students conduct Partner Reading and Partner Summarizing with subsequent paragraphs and use the strategy the teacher modeled.

The Bilingual Cooperative Integrated Reading and Composition (BCIRC) (Calderón et al., 1998) has teachers read aloud in Spanish or in English during the allocated language time to model comprehension strategies, but it also teaches students how to use the strategies as they do Partner Reading. BCIRC teaches students what to do before reading, during reading, and after reading a text thus building comprehension and mastering the material by using a variety of cognitive strategies, including summarization, prediction, story grammar, graphic organizers, partner reading, and mental imagery. The BCIRC model is one of the handful of reading programs that is evidence-based and is included in the What Works Clearinghouse. The Reading Wings/Alas Para Leer bilingual reading programs (Slavin & Madden, 2001) for upper elementary and middle schools nest the following strategies into cooperative learning: listening comprehension through Think-Alouds, story structure analysis, vocabulary building, partner reading, story retelling, spelling, story-related writing, and partner checking strategies. In each of the cooperative methods cited here, students are given specific guidance in how to help a partner or teammate learn the content and develop a strategy. ExC-ELL, whose roots are based in BCIRC, has refined and honed these cognitive strategies to pair Partner Reading with immediate Partner Summarization, Think-Alouds to analyze grammar, text features, and structure. In ExC-ELL, cooperative learning plays a central role in introducing strategy instruction to students.

Self-Regulation/Debriefing/Metacognition

Metacognitive strategies typically grouped under the term self-regulation can be taught and used as reading comprehension strategies (Paris & Paris, 2001). In one sense, all mindful use of cognitive reading comprehension strategies is self-regulation, but self-regulated learning goes beyond this to touch on motivation, self-evaluation, and other learning efforts. A large body of research has shown the achievement benefits of self-regulatory strategies such as goal setting (Schunk & Swartz, 1993), using self-verbalization to talk oneself through a problem (Schunk & Cox, 1986), and self-monitoring by recording one's progress (Zimmerman, Bonner, & Kovach, 1996).

ExC-ELL teachers are taught to debrief with their students after each instructional and cooperative learning event to clarify, anchor knowledge and strategies, and think about improving their strategies for next time.

Writing Builds Comprehension

There is evidence writing to learn can contribute to improved reading comprehension and content learning (Boscolo & Mason, 2001; Pugalee, 2002; Spanier, 1992). Both discussion of texts and the production of texts are viewed as equally important to developing content-area literacy and learning. Effective writing instruction means giving ELs frequent opportunities to write, accompanied by feedback and ample opportunities to revise and edit, along with guidance in how to do so. Instead of dictations, short-answer writing strategies, and other similar tasks that limit writing practice, ELs need explicit strategies for writing associated with different types of texts.

Using the ExC-ELL method, teachers have students write to a text-based prompt after they have acquired critical Tier 2 vocabulary, read and summarized the text, created text-based questions, participated in cooperative learning or class discussions. This process provides the vocabulary, structure, model, and background needed to be successful with such writing.

Assessment

Assessment should work in partnership with teaching and learning, particularly as it relates to differentiated learning and differentiated assessment practices (Gottlieb, 2006; Tierney & Readence, 2000). In the delivery of classroom instruction, language proficiency standards and academic content standards must merge and commingle if we are to assess EL progress (Gottlieb, 2006). ExC-ELL practitioners learn about the following assessment strategies to use in conjunction with their teaching: performance assessment, portfolios, anecdotal records, and for assessing team products, cooperative learning methods, and writing. Checklists and rubrics are also used to help students practice self-assessment and peer assessment. This provides the basis for formal and informal data analysis and a base for moving forward with future lessons.

Monitoring

As students proceed through all 12 components, the teacher is constantly monitoring student performance. The teacher can monitor and record the type of vocabulary, fluency, and comprehension during partner reading, accuracy of verbal summarization, and learning progressions on content mastery and content-based writing.

Three Basic Premises Guiding These Lessons

Premise 1—100% Student Interaction. A feature that is perhaps the most critical for EL success is the continuous constant production on oracy and literacy tasks. For every instructional and learning event, the students must produce and practice until there is evidence of mastery. For example, a teacher uses specific techniques such as "turn to your partner," choral responses, Cooperative Learning strategies for peer learning, and others to ensure all ELs are talking and practicing the new words; instead of Round-Robin Reading, teachers use Partner Reading and Partner Summarizing to ensure 100% time on reading for all students; instead of calling on one student for an answer, teachers use the Numbered-Heads-Together strategy, where all students discuss the answer and one number is called to represent the group. This method ensures that all students prepare each other to respond successfully.

Premise 2—Semantic Awareness. A school, classroom, and learning environment must be permeated with a mindset that ELs are learning words minute by minute. For example, a principal in a middle school ends her announcements with "the word of the day." She states the word twice, gives a definition, and uses it in a sentence. As she walks around school the rest of the day, the students stop her and give their own sentence with the word of the day. Another example is when teachers meet in interdisciplinary teams and identify sets of high utility words that cut across all content areas, and polysemous words such as *table, cell, power, radical,* and so on. They plan which words to teach on a weekly basis to ensure more than 35 exposures/encounters with a word in a variety of contexts.

Premise 3—The Explicit Teaching of Reading Comprehension. Explicit instruction for developing reading comprehension skills and strategies can be applied to other reading situations (Slavin & Madden, 2001; Tierney & Readence, 2000) such as content reading. The National Reading Panel (2000) found that comprehension strategy instruction, as opposed to comprehension skill practice (e.g., traditional skill work such as identifying main idea, cause-effect, fact-opinion) was important for students' reading growth. The features of explicit teaching include the following:

- **Relevance**: Students are made aware of the purpose of the skill or strategy—the why, when, how, and where of the strategy.
- **Definition**: Students are informed as to how to apply the skills by making public the skill or strategy, modeling its use, discussing its range of utility, and illustrating what it is not.
- **Guided practice**: Students are given feedback on their own use of the strategy or skill.
- **Self-regulation**: Students are given opportunities to try out the strategy for themselves and develop ways to monitor their own use of the strategy or skill.
- **Gradual release of responsibility**: The teacher initially models and directs the students' learning; as the lesson progresses, the teacher gradually gives more responsibility to the student.
- **Application**: Students are given the opportunity to try their skills and strategies in independent learning situations, including nonschool tasks (National Reading Panel, 2000).

First Steps in Lesson Design for Integrating Vocabulary, Reading, and Content

Teachers use the first five components of the lesson plan as described in the beginning of this chapter to plan their lesson. First, they select the *standard or objective*. This helps them to do backward planning, where the outcome is determined first, then the lesson is designed. To measure the outcome, *student assessments* are selected or developed next. Once the outcomes are determined, teachers preview the Mentor Text to select vocabulary to teach before, during, and after reading; eliminate unnecessary information; and segment the text for orchestrating daily activities. This is called *parsing* the text. The Mentor Text can be a textbook chapter, a math word problem, a science lab worksheet, a long story, anything the students are about to read. Not all texts need parsing. Some are short enough already. However, when it is "impossible to cover" all the information in a chapter or a whole book, it is wise and practical to parse. In this instance then, parsing entails choosing the portion of the Mentor Text that is the most important and contains the maximum amount of content students must master. At times, this means some paragraphs and pieces of text are left out. It is better that students learn basic concepts profoundly from key paragraphs than try to cover too much superficially.

You will notice that we use the term *Mentor Text.* A Mentor Text is just that: a text that models, teaches, mentors the reader in content, vocabulary usage, structure, mechanics, or purpose. A Mentor Text does not need to do all of these at once, but judicious selection and explicit instruction of the concepts and standards modeled by a Mentor Text will help all learners see appropriate usage and flow.

The next chapter lays out how to select and teach vocabulary that is appropriate not just for ELs, but also for all students in a classroom. Subsequently, the chapter on reading comprehension uses questions to think about what the focus will be for a particular lesson and what to do before, during, and after students read a selection. The ensuing chapters provide lessons for math, science, language arts, and interdisciplinary units.

Summary

✓ There are three basic premises that guide instruction for ELs and low-level readers: (1) ensuring 100% oral use, reading practice, and written production of new words and concepts; (2) establishing a mindset of semantic awareness; and (3) the explicit teaching of reading comprehension skills germane to each content area.

✓ There are five components that assist teachers of science, social studies, math, and language arts in planning lessons that integrate vocabulary and reading comprehension skill development.

✓ There are 12 components that assist content teachers in planning the delivery of their content and the way students will interact with that content to process and learn critical information.

✓ There is a strong research base for each of the 12 components. While it is essential for teachers to use the 12 components, empirical studies indicate that they are adjustable to a teacher's curricula, grade level, teacher creativity, and subject area.

3

Vocabulary Development

Selecting for High-Impact Usage and Comprehension

"Wow, look at all those words, Mister. So much. Do we have to know them all?"

—Evelina, second year in U.S. Russian-speaking
English Learner upon discovering the Oxford English
Dictionary in her school's Media Center

Preplanning and Selecting What to Teach: Words, Phrases, and More

The precursor to reading in content areas is preteaching vocabulary. The first step for preteaching vocabulary words and phrases is to know your Mentor Text and your students. You need to be highly familiar with the Mentor Text you will be using for your lesson, and you will also need to know the ELD (English Language Development) levels of your students so that you can reach them where they are and help them to both learn the content and the language of the content. This means reading or rereading the text each time you plan to teach the lesson. Your students and their needs are different from year to year. Consider your students, their levels, and the concepts you wish to work on for the lesson. Also consider what you expect your students to return to you as proof that they own the content.

In this process, you will note that we use the terms *Mentor Text* and *Parsing*. A Mentor Text is any text that students will need to comprehend and later delve into to show that comprehension; a model because it serves as an example for their own writing later. It may be a chapter in a textbook or a novel, but can also be a poem, lyrics to a song, a word problem, a play, dialogue from a video clip, or even a set of directions.

We use the word Parsing to indicate two activities. The first is preplanning. The teacher reviews and decides how much to teach, what words should be pretaught, and what grammatical features or structure should be featured as part of the lesson. The second part is to help focus the students. The teacher explicitly indicates how much text will be covered in the immediate lesson so that students know where to direct their energies.

The preplanning part consists of the following: (1) Deciding how much to focus on for the immediate lesson—how much time is needed to adequately cover the text, vocabulary needed for facility with reading comprehension, classroom discussions, writing, and other lesson strategies. (2) Selecting the appropriate Tier 1 or 2 vocabulary or phrases that need to be pretaught before reading begins. This also includes what Tier 3 words or phrases need to be focused on while reading or after reading. (3) Deciding what grammar, text structure, text features, or other elements you need to highlight as part of the lesson. Finally, (4) how will students prove to you that they comprehend the content and how will you judge that content.

For students, this simply means that you the teacher have told the students how much of the text that day's lesson will focus on. Students then know that all questions, summarizing, and discussions will focus on that piece of text until otherwise indicated.

Before, During, and After

Before going much further, we want to clarify a few things about teaching vocabulary. As the keystone to comprehension, vocabulary is an important component to teach students. However, it is not a one-and-done strategy. Neither is it a strategy that happens only at the beginning of reading. Later in this chapter, we focus on preteaching Tier 2 vocabulary; however, preteaching is only one component and is a precursor to getting students started reading. Vocabulary must be taught before, during, and after reading. It should be done during cooperative learning strategies, during the writing process, or during any discussion or strategy that lends itself to helping students understand the richness, power, and specificity of the correct word. Later we will discuss the subcategories of vocabulary that should be considered when parsing a text. Anytime is a good time for a vocabulary lesson, but it is not the only thing that needs to be taught. All vocabulary should be carefully and judiciously considered based upon your students' language development level, the text your students are about to read, and what language (words) you want your students to return to you as proof that they understand the content you have presented to them.

Selecting Words or Phrases to Teach

The process for the selection of words to preteach was based on research by Beck and colleagues (Beck, McKeown, & Kucan, 2002) as well as on the work of the Vocabulary Improvement Project (Carlo, August, & Snow, 2005), the BCIRC study (Calderón, Hertz-Lazarowitz, & Slavin, 1998), and the Transition from Spanish into English study (Calderón, August, et al., 2005). Beck and colleagues have developed a systematic method of selecting vocabulary to teach to students. Vocabulary is grouped into three tiers, and words in Tier 2 are those targeted for instruction. Tier 2 words include (1) words that have importance and utility (they are characteristic of mature language users and appear frequently across a variety of domains); (2) words that have instructional potential (words that can be worked with in a variety of ways so that students can build rich representations of them and their connections to other words and concepts; and (3) words for which students already have conceptual understanding (words for which students understand the general concept, but provide precision and specificity in describing the concept). Tier 1 words are words English-speaking students already know, and Tier 3 words are words students are unlikely to know, but are also words that are not frequently used across a variety of domains. The approach to teaching the words in each tier is predicated on four dimensions: nature of the word (is it concrete, or can it be demonstrated), its cognate status, depth of word meaning, and utility (Beck et al., 2002).

Tier 1 Words for ELs

We take it for granted that native English speakers know most Tier 1 words, based upon age and grade level, but this is not the case

---

TIER 1

Words that ELs need for everyday speech, for academic conversations and explanations, and for scaffolding more complicated text.

- ✓ Basic words for which students know concept and label in the primary language but need English label (e.g., *find, search, guest, tooth, answer*).
- ✓ Simple idioms are basic expressions that ELs are unlikely to know (e.g., *make up your mind; let's hit the books; once upon a time; sit up*).
- ✓ Connectors (e.g., *so, if, then, next, last*).

---

for ELs. Many Tier 1 words may be unknown to ELs and are key to the comprehension of a written passage. Newcomers may know even less. For Tier 1 words, ELs typically know the concept in their primary language, but not the label in English. For example, a Tier 1 word might be *butterfly.* This is a word that English Learners may not know, but it can be easily taught during a text presentation and discussion by pointing to a picture of a butterfly and asking the students to say it three times. Another Tier 1 word might be *bug.* Words like *bug* (insect) or *march* (move like a soldier) may be easily instructed during text discussion by pointing to a picture of a *bug* or *marching* in place. Caution however is warranted when using pictures. The picture must explicitly convey the contextual meaning of the word, or it fails to provide the correct definition. Many of these Tier 1 words are polysemous (have multiple meanings), and as such, merit further instruction. This is accomplished in oral language activities that follow the text discussion (Calderón et al., 2005).

There are some Tier 1 words that cannot be demonstrated and are not polysemous, but students will need to know them also (e.g., *cousin*). A simple explanation of the word's meaning during the story reading will suffice, or if the teacher and students are bilingual, a translation is sufficient.

Tier 1 words are not limited to single words. In fact, Tiered Vocabulary is not limited to individual words. For that reason, at times, you will see us use "words or phrases" or "words/phrases" and if we do not add the actual word *phrases*, mentally add it in yourself. Words are not single entities. They should always be analyzed for what they contextually mean. A good habit to have when parsing a text for words to teach is to look at the words to the left and right of the word you think should be taught. Ask yourself, "Is this word working alone in this text, or is it part of a cluster?" For instance, the word *due* has the meaning of "expected or planned at a certain time." However, the word cluster *due to* means "because of," and a phrase such as *due diligence* means to handle with a standard of care and attention.

Furthermore, simple idioms to native speakers and everyday expressions (e.g., *make up your mind; let's hit the books; once upon a time*) are also Tier 1 words/phrases, and teachers will need to explain the word meaning to students. Some Tier 1 words are cognates with a language like Spanish (*family/familia; preparation/preparación*). The cognates in this category consist of words that are high-frequency words in Spanish and English, and they do not require substantial instruction because students know the word meanings in Spanish. While teaching or reading, the teacher merely states the English cognate, and students provide the Spanish cognate, or the teacher provides the English cognate, and the students say both the English word and Spanish cognate. False cognates also need to be pointed out by the teacher *rope/ropa, soap/sopa* and the correct translation given, that is, *rope/soga, soap/jabón*. (See Step 5 of the "7 Steps for Preteaching Vocabulary" later in this chapter for further discussion.) The word *assist* is usually translated as *asistir*, but the correct translation is *atender*, and *attend* means *asistir*. Yet *asistencia* means *assistance*, but *attendance* is not *atendencia* (this is not a Spanish word). Confusing enough? We call these *polysemous cognates*. They can be either true or false cognates, depending on the context.

Tier 2 Words for ELs

These are words and phrases that have importance and utility because they are in grade-level texts. Unfortunately, these do not receive as much attention as Tier 1 and Tier 3 words because ESL/ELD teachers typically teach Tier 1, and mainstream teachers focus on Tier 3 (content specific) words. It's our hypothesis that the lack of explicit instruction of Tier 2 words is what keeps ELs from moving on to Tier 3 words and thus developing reading comprehension of content texts. Furthermore, lack of understanding the Tier 2 words that nest, support, and most often are in the definitions of Tier 3 words prevent ELs from comprehending those vital Tier 3 subject words. (As an example, later in this chapter we talk about the polysemy of the Tier 3 word *translation*.) If students don't understand the definition, how can they possibly understand the concept?

Tier 2 words can be incorporated into all lessons in a variety of ways, so students can build rich representations of them and make connections to content words and concepts. These are also words for which students understand the general concept but need to learn to provide precision and specificity in describing the concept.

TIER 2

Criteria for Identifying Tier 2 Words and Phrases

✓ Importance and utility: Words characteristic of mature language users appear frequently across a variety of domains and primarily fall in these subcategories:

- Information processing words
- Polysemous words
- Sophisticated words for specificity or precision
- Connectors, transition words
- Cognates and false cognates
- Phrasal clusters
- Idioms, metaphors, similes, puns, and collocations
- Sentence and question starters

✓ Conceptual understanding: words for which students understand the general concept but provide precision and specificity of the concept.

A Few Examples
Connectors: Cause and Effect

because, due to, as a result, since, for this reason, therefore, in order to, so that, thus . . .

Transitions: Contrast

although, however, in contrast, nevertheless, on the other hand, while . . .

Clusters

due to, get along with, get down, will have to, should have, would like to, a soft spot for, in a state . . .

Polysemy

Some of the most troublesome words for ELs have multiple meanings based upon context. It is important to teach words like *trunk, leg, table, state, power, right,* and *left,* because ELs typically know only one meaning, and that meaning may not be relevant to the context or content in which it is found.

Many Tier 2 words are those tiny words that make comprehension difficult for ELs, such as *so, at, into, within, by, if, then*. Others are sometimes clustered to connote certain usage, constructs, or "ways of talking about school stuff," as one teacher calls them. They are also called transition words. These are helpful to compare and contrast, to describe or give examples.

In addition, other Tier 2 words are cognates. In this Tier, they are high-frequency words in Spanish or any other Romance language and low-frequency words in English. ELs whose first language shares cognates with English will have a head start with these words. Words in Spanish parallel words in English, such as *digestion/digestion, coincidence/coincidencia, industrious/industrioso,* and *fortunate/afortunado*. Depending upon the learner's primary language development, Spanish speakers may know both the concept and an approximation of the label in English. If they don't know the meaning in either language, both can be taught together. This category also includes less-common idioms and metaphors that are key to making inferences.

Tier 3 Words for Els

Numerous Tier 3 words are cognates because they are specific to certain content areas (e.g., *osmosis, photosynthesis, translation*). However, students may not know the actual concept or process; therefore, they need to be pretaught along with the concept after they read them in context. Sometimes, the students may have partial knowledge of a concept or word (fractions) and need details or specificity. If possible, Tier 3 words that are not demonstrable or are cognates can be translated or briefly explained in the first language. Or even better, help them learn the Tier 2 words that form the definition of the Tier 3 word. In this category, we also include others that may not be essential to understanding the main points of the text. These can be explained briefly to the students, but they don't have to master these words.

Cognates and polysemous words can be either Tier 1, 2, or 3 or at times, all three. It depends on the difficulty of the word or the background knowledge of the student. Similarly, selecting words for the three tiers will also depend on the subject, grade level, and student background knowledge. *There are no lists for Tiers 1, 2, and 3.* Each classroom will be different. Each group of students will be different. Each text will be different. Each will require an analysis of the words to be taught before, during, and after reading.

It is crucial to preselect words to teach before, during, and after reading to focus on the contextual concepts from the standards and

TIER 3

Low-Frequency Words in English

Content specific words that are limited to specific subjects: social studies, math, language arts, or science. Although they are low-frequency words, they are very important for understanding content.

For instance: *geology, isotope, organism, osmosis, vertical, format, divisor, hyperbole.*

- ✓ The above examples are all cognates; words in two or more languages that sound almost the same or are spelled the same (for instance in English, Spanish, and French, we find words such as *telephone/teléfono/téléphone; the radio, el radio, le radio; education/ la educación/l'éducation*).
- ✓ Literate Spanish speakers have a great advantage over monolingual English speakers with Tier 3 words because many cognates are high-frequency words in Spanish, but low-frequency words in English (e.g., *coincidence/coincidencia, absurd/absurdo, concentrate/concéntrate, and fortunate/afortunado*).
- ✓ However, students may need to learn the concept or specificity for some cognates (e.g., *democracy/democracia*).

Word Preteaching Checklist

Tier 2 word? No? Stop! If it is a Tier 1 word, teach it at a different time (maybe while doing a Think-Aloud) using a gesture, picture, or text feature. If it is a Tier 3 word, the definition is in the glossary, a footnote or even as an intratext definition.
   Yes, this is a Tier 2 word! Ask:

- ✓ Is it *critical* to the understanding of what they are about to read?
- ✓ Is it *imperative* to the understanding of the concept?
- ✓ Is it *critically* important to the discipline?
- ✓ It is *vitally* important to this unit.
- ✓ Would it probably appear on a test?
- ✓ Do I want to hear it in their Partner Summaries?
- ✓ Do I want to see it in a later writing assignment?
- ✓ Does it appear often in this text?

If the answer to any of the above is no, then STOP and choose a different time and method to teach this word.

basic knowledge that will make a difference in the student's success. As the students delve into the text, there will be other words you might not have even thought about. These can be collected and pretaught the following day, or they can be taught quickly without interrupting the reading too long. The following section describes ways teachers and students like to conduct word study strategies in the context of learning content and preparing for exams.

Polysemy Across the Tiers

Polysemous words are found in all three tiers. Tier 1 polysemous words for example are *saw, leg, hand, body*. Yes, these are common everyday words that ELs should know at the appropriate age and grade levels. However, what does *saw* mean, when used as a verb? The past tense of to see, correct? Yes, but what about in this sentence? *The lumberjack saw his saw near the sawmill and began to saw the lumber.* In this instance, *saw* is the past tense of to see, a compound noun and a tool, plus an action meaning to cut.

Content-specific words are equally fraught with polysemy. Take the word *translation.* In language arts or social studies content, *translation* is the process of changing words from one language into a different language. However, in math, *translation* is a term used in geometry to describe a function that moves an object a certain distance. For science, *translation* is the process of synthesizing the sequence of a messenger RNA (mRNA) molecule into a sequence of amino acids. Perhaps an EL will understand the contextual meaning in language arts or social studies class, but will the EL understand the meaning in math or science without understanding the Tier 2 words that make up the definition?

Criteria for Selecting the Words and Phrases to Teach

As we have trained teachers, they have helped us develop a process for selecting which words to teach. Begin with Tier 3 words that connect with the content of your class. Reserve these Tier 3 words and phrases for students to decipher and learn while reading; yes, they are important but can be taught while reading, or are typically in the glossary, diagrams, footnotes, or have intra-text definitions. For example, the word *ichthyologist* may well be immediately followed by the explanation "a scientist that studies fish." In addition, they may require Tier 2 context clues and will take too much time for preteaching.

Focus on Tier 2 words and phrases for preteaching. Try to cluster as much as possible. By way of explanation, a phrasal cluster is a group of words that have a different meaning as a group than they do as each individual word's meaning when seen separately. For instance, "on the other hand" is made up of four individual Tier 1 words. However, when you put them together as a cluster, they have a different meaning. Therefore, teach them as a cluster.

Verbal clusters as well should be looked at very carefully. We discussed this concept above briefly with the word *due* when combined with other words. There is a great deal of difference between *due* and *due to*—"The paper was given a lower grade *due to* being turned in two days after it was *due*." Note the two different meanings of the word due used within one sentence.

Once you have your list, underline the five or six words/phrases that you want to preteach. Now, for each of the words, ask yourself the following questions: *"Is this word critical to the understanding of what they are about to read? Is it critical to the understanding of the concept? Would it probably appear on a test? Is it critically important to the discipline? To this unit? Do I want to hear it in their Partner Summaries? Do I want to see it in their Exit Pass or in a writing assignment? Will it appear several times in this or the following pieces of the text my students will be reading? If the answer is yes, then it is a good candidate for preteaching."*

Preteaching Vocabulary

Preteaching vocabulary is the keystone to comprehension and the precursor to reading. Before students read a text or a teacher reads a text aloud to the students or a teacher lectures, it is vital to preteach five or six words (phrases) that are key to comprehending that text or lecture. There may be many words ELs do not know in each subject area. Therefore, the selection of those five to six words to preteach in all content classrooms needs special attention. Focusing on Tier 2 words, when needed teachers can select one or two words from each Tier 1 or 3 if crucial to the comprehension of the text, to aide students' progress through a textbook or combination of reading, discussions, lectures, and summarizing of content.

Preteaching vocabulary is a seven-step process. It is different from the process used by Beck and colleagues because these steps integrate second-language strategies.

---

7 Steps of Preteaching Vocabulary

2 minutes TOTAL for each word

Step 1 Teacher says the word (or phrase) and asks students to repeat the word 3 times.

Step 2 Teacher states the word in context from text. Use the sentence that contains the word you are preteaching.

Step 3 Teacher provides the dictionary definition.

Step 4 Teacher provides student-friendly definition.

Step 5 Teacher highlights grammar, spelling, polysemy, etc.

Step 6 Students engage in a teacher-provided sentence starter or frame using the target vocabulary for 60 seconds.

Step 7 Teacher informs students how/when to use the word later.

Notes

Steps 1–5 and 7 = 1 minute

Step 6 = 1 full minute

Total = 2 minutes per word

Students are NOT writing, drawing, guessing, or looking anything up in a dictionary during this strategy.

Step 1: Teacher says the word (or phrase) and asks students to repeat the word three times

Rationale: Saying the word three (3) or more times helps students with pronunciation and avoids fossilization of mispronunciation.

Variations: The three repetitions can be consecutive or ping-pong style with the teacher for those words that might need more specific pronunciation refinement. Another variation is to have students say the word in a fun way 3 times, or whisper to their partners.

Step 2: Teacher states the word in context from text. Use the sentence that contains the word you are preteaching

Rationale: Taking the word and sentence directly from the text provides the context that helps students recall the meaning of the word when they are reading. This also provides immediate familiarity and success with the whole sentence later when students Partner Read/Summarize.

Step 3: Teacher provides the dictionary definition

Rationale: The dictionary definition provides a connection to the academic language students will need to cultivate. The teacher must look up and use the definition relevant to the text, using a grade-level appropriate dictionary.

Caution: During preteaching, students *do not* look up words in the dictionary. It takes too long, and they invariably select the wrong meaning. Neither at this time do students guess what the word means or tell us what they think it means. This as well takes too long and frequently is contextually or completely wrong.

Step 4: Teacher provides student-friendly definition

Rationale: Some dictionary definitions are much more difficult than the word itself. Therefore, in Step 4, the teacher provides a student-friendly definition or an example to make sure all students grasp the meaning.

Caution: Do not ask students to provide the student-friendly definition. It will take too much time and they might get it wrong.

Step 5: Teacher highlights grammar, spelling, polysemy, etc.

Rationale: Sometimes teachers want students to know something special about the word: It's a noun, it's a verb, it's a polysemous word, it has a cognate, or it has a different meaning in a different subject—but the teacher must emphasize the explicit meaning for this lesson. Step 5 is not the time to do a grammar mini lesson. That comes later.

Caution: In this step, highlight only *one* key item.

Step 6: Students engage in a teacher-provided sentence starter or frame using the target vocabulary for 60 seconds

Rationale: This is where 100% of the students practice the word aloud for 1 full minute (60 seconds). The teacher provides a frame or starter containing *the target vocabulary*. Students practice the word using *complete sentences* in pairs. Pairs must be prearranged, which might mean rearranging the class for this purpose taking into consideration the English proficiency levels of each student. For example, pair a high and a medium or a native and an EL. While the pairs are practicing, the teacher is roaming amongst the students collecting formative assessment data.

Caution: (1) The more concise the sentence frame or starter, the better. (2) Correction is kept to a minimum. Teachers use a timer to help keep the process moving along and on time.

Examples: Target vocabulary: *tasked with*. Sentence frame, "After school I am *tasked with* _____."

Target vocabulary: *would like to*. Sentence frame, "After school I *would like to* _____."

Step 7: Teacher informs students how/when to use the word in Partner Reading/Summaries, Exit Passes, or later writing assignments

Rationale: This step is also oral—no writing, no drawing, no copying from board. This step is only to inform students when and where they can expect to see and use the word. For example, in their reading, in their peer oral summaries, and later in their writing, homework, essays, lab reports, exit pass, etc.

Here is an example script of how teaching the word *effect* might look through the 7-steps:

Step 1 *Teacher*: "Say EFFECT 3 times." *Students*: "EFFECT, EFFECT, EFFECT"

Step 2 *Teacher*: "In our reading today, you will read this sentence, 'Fortunately, we can prepare for some of the negative EFFECTs on our well-being.'"

Step 3 *Teacher*: "The dictionary definition is, 'The result or consequence of something.'"

Step 4 *Teacher*: "Here is an example, 'Two cups of coffee in the morning have a big EFFECT on me—I can't sleep at night!'"

Step 5 *Teacher*: "It is a cognate. If you speak Spanish you might recognize it—*efecto*. But in English we spell it with two 'fs' and no 'o.'"

Step 6 *Teacher*: "Use this sentence frame for your sentences, '_____ has had a big effect on my life recently.'" *Students*: Ping-ponging back and forth for 60 minutes using the target word in complete sentence.

Step 7 *Teacher*: "Use effect in your partner reading and summaries, plus today's Exit Pass."

---

5 Steps of Preteaching Vocabulary to Newcomers and Lower Level ELs

2 minutes TOTAL for each word

Step 1 Teacher says the word (or phrase) and asks students to repeat the word 3 times.

Step 2 Teacher states the word in context from text. Use the sentence that contains the word you are preteaching.

Step 3 Teacher provides student-friendly definition.

Step 4 Students engage in a teacher-provided sentence starter or frame using the target vocabulary for 60 seconds.

Step 5 Teacher informs students how/when to use the word later.

Notes

Students are NOT writing, drawing, guessing, or looking anything up in a dictionary during this strategy.

Academic Language: The closer the learners get to a higher language proficiency level, start to bring in the dictionary definition. Students need modelling and familiarity with academic language as soon as possible.

Grammar, spelling, phonics polysemy: Add this step back in when most effective or important to your lesson. Choose only one concept to highlight.

30 Seconds at the start: At this level, starting with 30 seconds and moving up to 45 then 60 seconds in a few weeks is acceptable.

Scaffolding: At this level, heavy support is needed. Students might simply need to repeat what a higher ELD level or native speaking peer says.

5 Steps for Preteaching Vocabulary to Newcomers

For Newcomers, SIFE students, the 7 Steps are modified into the following 5 Steps.

Step 1   Teacher says the word (or phrase) and asks students to repeat the word 3 times.

Step 2   Teacher states the word in context from text. Use the sentence that contains the word you are preteaching.

Step 3   Teacher provides student-friendly definition.

However: The closer the learners get to a higher ELD level or near the end of level one, start to bring in the dictionary definition. Students need modelling and familiarity with academic language as soon as possible.

For the *grammar, spelling, phonics polysemy* step, add that in when most effective or important to your lesson. Again, however, choose only one concept to highlight.

Step 4   Students engage in a teacher-provided sentence starter or frame using the target vocabulary.

Note: At the Newcomer level, starting with 30 seconds and moving up to 45 then 60 seconds in a few weeks is acceptable. Also, at this level, heavy support is needed. Students might simply need to repeat what a higher ELD level or native speaking peer says.

Step 5   Teacher informs students how/when to use the word in Partner Reading/Summaries, Exit Passes, or later writing assignments.

Variations for 100% Student Participation

There are many other ways of getting students engaged with a word. It does not always have to be a ping pong strategy. Usage of these variations are for occasional use and must be highly monitored to ensure that there is 100% engagement. Each student should supply at least 5 or 6 examples during the ping pong. Here are a few other examples to help learners think about specificity when using adjectives, verbs, or concepts:

- "Which of these things would be *integers*, is a positive number or a fraction, a negative number, a decimal or a percent? Answer in a complete sentence and use the word."
- Affirm or Deny: Fill in the blank and repeat the correct sentence, "*Yes/No* _____ *is/is not the name of a U.S. President.*" James Monroe, Martin Sheen, Benjamin Franklin, Thomas Jefferson

---

Vocabulary: On the Run

Concrete and Specific Concepts

Some words and phrases can be explicitly and easily demonstrated with a gesture, picture, or realia (i.e., *smile, cattle, yarn*)

Metacognitive Thinking

"Oh, that word looks like … but it has '-ed' on the end. Hmm, that usually means it's in the past."
"Okay, I know part of this word 'necessary,' and I know 'un' means 'not,' so this must mean 'not needed.'"

Prior Knowledge

"Great, can you use a word we just used to summarize or answer that?"
"Look at this word. We know a similar word …."

Cognates (if you know them)

"Hey, this word in Spanish is … but we say it in English like this … Repeat it three times with me."

When teachers use strategies such as these to preteach vocabulary, they are also teaching or reviewing other skills, concepts, and/or metacognitive strategies. With the example of the word *integer*, students need to listen carefully, compare two responses, and choose the most appropriate one. They have to think quickly, make inferences, and respond. The teacher can ask for complete sentence responses, where ELs can practice answering long strands of discourse, scaffolded by the teacher's phrases. This ensures appropriate answers, the use of *would be,* and other more sophisticated patterns. (A positive number *would be* an example of an integer.) Responding in complete sentences creates a sense of confidence and self-efficacy in the ELs as their responses become increasingly sophisticated.

Optimizing Your Preteaching Time

Frequently teachers feel that they *must* preteach the Tier 3 words, because they will be on the test. This is valid; however, preteaching a Tier 3 word may not be the most productive use of the 7-Steps timeframe. If you must teach Tier 3, and you want to use the 7 Steps, start your planning with Step 6. This is the step where you, the teacher, provides a sentence frame using the target word. To check the viability of using your Tier 3 word for preteaching, start by creating the sentence starter or frame you want your students to use for their 60 seconds (or 6 times each) of practice with the target word in a complete sentence. Does your sentence stem provide enough variety? If not, use a different strategy to teach the word during or after reading. Take the word *osmosis* for example. How many different times in those 60 seconds can students use osmosis in a complete sentence? As a pretaught word, not many. Even after learning the concept, it isn't that easy. Therefore, *osmosis*, while an important concept word, needs to be taught through partner reading and partner summarizing (see next two chapters on reading).

Strategy Process Notes: The 7 Steps for Preteaching Vocabulary

At www.ExC-ELL.com, we have a Lesson Integration Tool. Use the tool to script out your five words or phrases before teaching them. Share these words with a colleague who is also doing the same and peer review each other's selections. Also available on our website is the WISEcard, which we recommend to use for self-reflection, lesson review. Simply video tape yourself doing the 7 Steps and then review the video with the WISEcard as your own personal coaching session.

When first learning the 7 Steps, start with two words per day or subject, then the following week add another subject or increase to four words or phrases. Soon you will be up to the recommended five per day per subject. Use a timer for yourself and the students. We have found that the biggest detractor from this strategy is when teachers take too much time for preteaching. It will take practice to keep the time down to 2 minutes per word: 1 minute for you and 1 minute for them for a *total* of 10 minutes for those five words. Resist the urge to have every student share out their Step 6 sentence. If you must have a share out, limit it to one example per word.

When you first introduce this new strategy (or any of the strategies we discuss) to your students, display and discuss the steps with your students. Have them practice the steps several times the first few times, as they are learning the routine too. Discuss why you are doing this new process with your students. Remember to debrief with them. Ask them after they have practiced the strategy a few times, "How is this helping you?"

Developing Vocabulary Through Discourse Around Text: During and After Reading

After preteaching, vocabulary is also developed during and after reading, in class discussions, and cooperative learning strategies through ongoing dialogue between the teacher and students about the text. Reading begins with the teacher reading aloud the first or a selected paragraph of a text. During the Read-Aloud, the teacher models making meaning and uses different types of self-questions, stopping at specific intervals to elicit discussion of meaning-making strategies and to teach more words "on the run." Different methods are used depending on the nature of the word (is it concrete, or can it be demonstrated?), its cognate status, depth of word meaning, and utility. The use of pantomime and gestures, showing pictures and real objects, and doing quick draws on the board can be used to quickly explain what a word means. As long as the action, picture, or realia is an explicit representation of the contextual meaning of the word, then these strategies work.

Questions can also help prompt students to talk about ideas using the target words. Questions must be carefully crafted ahead of time. Some questions elicit one-word responses or are likely to elicit only sparse responses. There are also questions that help students move from using just pictures and background knowledge to more elaborated responses tied to the text. Other questions call for more thinking and elaboration. Figure 6.1 (on page 98) is one example of a tool often distributed to the students for constructing and answering questions. In Chapter 6, we elaborate on student formulation of questions and strategies to facilitate deeper content comprehension and classroom debriefing for after reading and summarizing of the Mentor Text.

Teaching vocabulary is not an end in itself. It is only a precursor into reading, writing, and conducting rich discussions in every content area (Calderón & Soto, 2017). The importance of vocabulary, the number of words students need to learn, means that teachers need to provide powerful vocabulary instruction through a rich array of language experiences in listening, speaking, reading, and writing in all content areas. Student reading should immediately follow the preteaching of vocabulary. This will allow even more practice of the target vocabulary and will help to solidify comprehension and mastery of the pretaught words and phrases. In that vein, the next two chapters move forward with bridging vocabulary learning for reading comprehension and on into content consolidation strategies with the final goal of writing as proof of learning.

Summary

✓ Vocabulary must be explicitly taught to ELs if they are to catch up to grade-level standards.

✓ Vocabulary instruction must be firmly connected to and rooted in the text the students are about to read.

✓ Vocabulary instruction must also be part of a comprehensive language and literacy program across the content areas.

✓ It is important to preselect words to teach before, during, and after reading to focus on the most important concepts from the standards and basic knowledge that will make a difference in the students' test results.

✓ Explicit instruction on word knowledge consisting of phonemic, phonological, and morphemic awareness, decoding, and understanding of the multiple meanings of the words occurs in the context of teaching reading and using content texts.

✓ Language development is accelerated through reading, discussing, writing about texts—after Tier 1, 2, and 3 vocabulary has been explicitly taught.

4

Bridging Vocabulary and Reading

Conclusion 8-4: Literacy engagement is critical during the middle school grades. During these grades, students are required to read and learn from advanced and complex grade level texts. For ELs, this problem is acute because instructional support for long-term English learners tends to emphasize skills instead of dealing with the barriers to their motivation to learn, engagement in the classroom, and literacy engagement.

—National Academies of Sciences, Engineering, and Medicine (NAS, 2017)

Why All Middle and High School Teachers Are Reading Teachers

The first edition of our book *Teaching Reading to English Language Learners, Grades 6–12: A Framework for Improving Achievement in the Content Areas* described what we had learned up until then from being embedded in middle and high schools in New York City and Kauai. That 5-year research yielded the promising practices that the National Academies of Sciences, Engineering, and Medicine (NAS) now recommends in its latest publication on *Promoting Educational Success of Children and Youth Learning English: Promising Futures* (NAS, 2017).

The whole-school approach in New York City's and Kauai's schools demonstrated back in 2005–2009 that the eight recommendations in the NAS publication can result in great gains for ELs and all students in a school when ExC-ELL is implemented as a schoolwide whole-school initiative. Since then, we have seen the same positive results in schools in Virginia and Memphis, among other areas, where all core content teachers in a school are involved as well as site and central office administrators.

We will illustrate how the NAS recommendations are addressed in ExC-ELL and the recommendations we make for whole-school implementation. In this book, we regularly discuss the importance of *language development that embraces all facets of academic language* as a precursor into structured reading comprehension, cognitive processes, and writing instruction. In this chapter, we focus on the key components of reading that can be integrated into any subject area:

1. Preteaching of key vocabulary selected from the text students are about to read to learn content (Chapter 3)

2. Explicit teacher instruction and modeling of cognitive strategies for approaching the text features, text structures, and comprehension strategies that will help work through that specific text structure (Chapter 4)

3. Students read in pairs (or in triads when there is a Newcomer) to practice in a safe peer-on-peer environment for context reading fluency, comprehension, oral use of new vocabulary, discourse strings, summarization of the content they are learning, and social norms of peer interaction (Chapter 5)

4. Teacher–student opportunities for extended learning and practice of more language and content information processing (Chapter 6)

5. Student formulation of questions with peers for delving deeper into the text and working with close reading strategies (Chapter 5 or 6)

6. The use of motivating cooperative learning structures to test the questions students have written, explore language nuances, hypotheses, text evidence and counterevidence, while learning collaborative, communicative, and social-emotional skills (Chapter 5 or 6)

7. Different genre of text-based writing in teams first, then pairs, then independent writing (Writing Chapter 7)

8. The use of self-editing, revising, self-correction, and teacher-assessment processes that propel and motivate ELs in their efforts to integrate language, reading, writing, and content mastery (Writing Chapter 8)

Reading in the content areas has typically meant "reading to learn," as differentiated from beginning reading instruction, which has been referred to as "learning to read" (McKenna & Robinson, 1990). Content area literacy, or disciplinary literacy, for ELs refers to reading and writing to learn concepts from textbooks, novels, magazines, e-mail, electronic messaging, Internet materials, or Internet sites so they can keep up with their subject matter and pass the high-stakes tests.

For ELs, it correspondingly means learning to read these texts critically, forming opinions, and responding appropriately orally and later in writing. It means keeping up with all subjects and daily course work. It also means being part of the culture of the Internet to access the validity of said information, evaluate contents quickly, and synthesize information for various classes. English learners, like all other students, need to understand the languages of disciplines like biology, algebra, government, and English literature—for each is a different language unto itself. This is not easy to accomplish! Neither for ELs nor for their teachers! Nevertheless, this is what all teachers must strive for since ELs and other students need more literacy training than they can get in ESL or language arts classes alone.

Expository or informational texts also have their own organizational format. They vary considerably across subject matter. Scientists, mathematicians, historians, and linguists speak and write differently when explaining their disciplines. Explicit language and literacy-based strategies for each subject deepen ELs understanding of subject matter and help them develop a larger sophisticated content-specific vocabulary. Each discipline has its set of nomenclature and semantic preferences for nesting terminology. When students read and comprehend a subject, they can read more and use more language more effectively. However, decoding these various content variations must be explicitly taught using examples from the text students will be reading.

Whole-School Implementation

Throughout this book you will note that we regularly promote whole-school, whole staff, every educator in the building (or district to be honest) as responsible for the success of ELs. To that point, we understand and realize that many non-ESL content teachers will help in understanding why they are now literacy teachers as well as content teachers. Whole-school implementation includes administrators, instructional coaches, and other staff who work with students. When we present our ExC-ELL Institutes, many participants begin the sessions wondering the same. After helping them process through one of their lessons, focusing on the language of their content, with all the nuances of that same language as it explicitly relates to their subject, they begin to realize the need to teach the language of math, the language of science, and the language of social studies. By the end of the sessions, they realize that yes, they must become a reading and literacy teacher of their content.

In addition, a well-structured school where all teachers follow the same set of instructional strategies allows ELs and others to have that support they need: familiarity and reiteration. The processes, activities, and strategies, while completed or adapted in differing subjects, flow from one classroom and subject to another. These structures and strategies support the standards students are expected to demonstrate. Many educators need guidance and nurturing to see the benefits of whole-school implementation. With that in mind, we have addressed a few of the questions and beliefs of teachers learning how to be part of that whole-school community.

Working Through Outmoded Misconceptions: Conversations With the Whole Faculty

I Have Subject-Specific State Standards I Have to Teach

Content standards identify what students are expected to learn in the various disciplines as part of a good education. Content standards provide details for more general, abstract educational goals by specifying what thinking and performing capabilities students should master and what knowledge they should possess. Each subject has its own standards but requires similar reading skills. Standards in the subjects or disciplines so far have called for teaching with more informational texts, use of argumentative discourse based on text-cited evidence, close reading to find author's purpose, and details to support claims and counterclaims. The standards and types of text for each expected task guide the type of reading students need to prevail in learning the content.

In Chapter 5, we will delve deeper into reading each specific core content. However, there are basic text features, text structures, and grammatical and syntactical components of reading that are cross-curricular in nature. Content standards rely on the comprehension of these features, structures, and syntax to convey the subject matter content. These components of reading are the ones we need to be sure to highlight, model, and explicitly teach. Text features, text structures, mechanics, and syntax are what our students need to process to build meaning and assist with comprehension. As referenced above from the NAS, some of those barriers include these structures, features, and components: learning why a word is bolded or italicized, what a chart, diagram, or picture means for the reading, and being able to understand why the author wrote what he or she wrote and how it related to the learning at hand encourages engagement in the lesson. Teaching ELs and all students the function and usefulness of these components will help them to become more engaged in what they are reading and to successfully navigate the content and subject specificity they need.

Isn't Teaching Reading in the ESL/ELD Classroom Enough?

For years, the field of second-language teaching has espoused the concept of providing "comprehensible input" (Krashen, 1981), where teachers modify their speech and use visuals and other techniques to make instruction comprehensible to ELs. While it is important for ELs to understand the teacher, most ESL/ELD or sheltered content teachers simplify their language to the point where students are learning very few words, especially when it comes to academic language tied to subject matter. With few words, ELs will not be able to ever catch up with their peers in general education content classes. By themselves, ESL/ELD teachers cannot address reading skills in all the subject areas to prepare ELs to make an adequate transition to content classrooms. English language arts teachers alone can no longer provide the content-area literacy development students need to be college or career ready. Additionally, we have observed from our visits to vocational and technical courses that those texts are even more detailed, specific, and difficult than some Advance Placement courses!

It is quite likely most ELs were primarily exposed to narrative genre as commonly used in ESL/ELD or language arts. Their English as a second-language instruction might have consisted of only simple oral language patterns (e.g., "This is a … "; "I have a … ," and simple phrase responses) or reading short, choppy sentences. The words and grammatical structures that show rhetorical or narrative connections between ideas are often eliminated (Fillmore & Snow, 2002). English language learners' basic terminology, syntactical and discourse structures,

> Think about the challenge for ESL/ELD and sheltered instruction teachers as they attempt to provide (in their 30-minute blocks) rich vocabulary, syntactic structures, text features, text structures, and student practice with close reading as they apply all this to build reading comprehension for science, social studies, math, and literature!

and metacognitive processes for the subject matter you are teaching may be very limited or nonexistent. If so, then these students have a lot of catching up to do. Without additional reading and language development support from their mainstream content teachers, student comprehension remains at a shallow level—a surface comprehension level.

Just as it is vital for ELs to learn at least five words per subject per day, it is also important for ELs to learn text features, text structures, and reading comprehension strategies in every subject every day. Although ELs come with a variety of reading levels, teachers can help them sustain habits of close reading and reading stamina by following the instructional sequence previously outlined on page 50.

Not Enough Sheltering in General Education Classrooms When Not in an ESL/ELD Classroom

ELs are typically exposed to grade-level texts in their general education classrooms when not in an ESL/ELD pull-out setting, which is most of the day. This can work when core content teachers' instruction begins with parsing a text to provide an in-depth focus on a specific concept and includes as recommended by the NAS "explicit instruction focused on developing key aspects of literacy; developing academic language during content area instruction; providing support to make core content comprehensible" (2017). Not only does it improve general vocabulary, but also improves reading comprehension for all students. Furthermore we now know that even Newcomers can be challenged and succeed if teachers frontload by preteaching key words, then do a Think-Aloud to highlight text features and text structures. Instead of attempting to "cover" a lot of information, opportunities to *probe profoundly* into small meaningful chunks of grade-level texts help *all* students experience deep comprehension and critical thinking.

Why Phonics in Middle and High School?

Phonics programs in middle and high schools are fine as tools for Newcomers or ELs that have low literacy skills in their first language. They also help more advanced ELs and Long-Term ELs who struggle with spelling and writing. They need to hear and distinguish the phonemes (sounds) and morphemes (smallest units of meaning) of English to develop pronunciation, discourse, and writing dexterity. However, isolated and unconnected to text and content, phonics and decoding programs beyond 20 days have a downward spiral effect (Kamil, 2005). In other words, after 20 or so days of exposure to phonics only, there is no positive effect on students. Often, these programs focus only on sounds without word knowledge. For example, consider the multiplicity of the letter combination of *-ough*. This cluster of letters has 6 phonemes when combined, but have 14 when considered separately or in pairs; 20 in total. That means that students are parroting sounds devoid of meaning and sense to them.

Have you observed how some Long-Term ELs read very fluently when they read aloud? Nevertheless, when you ask them a question about what they read, they cannot answer? They probably had a large dose of phonics, yet not much attention was given to reading comprehension. Along with phonics instruction, students need opportunities to practice those decoding skills with real texts, followed by more word study, and real discussions with peers. Phonemic and phonetic awareness can be developed through Steps 3 and 5 of the 7-Step vocabulary strategy or the teacher's Think-Aloud.

Worksheets to Practice Grammar and Spelling

Worksheets, grammar exercises, or quietly answering the five questions at the end of a chapter are mainly busy work, but do not produce language or content learning. Do the ELs mainly get the answers from other students? What level of higher thinking skills are most of these questions? Remembering? These answers can easily be copied from the text. Instead, ELs could be formulating questions at higher levels after reading and summarizing a text with their partners. When students read aloud alternating sentences with a partner, stop at the end of a paragraph, and summarize aloud, they make meaning together. Partner reading anchors comprehension and the use of the new words that worksheets or grammar exercises cannot accomplish. When ELs or striving readers read silently or without a partner, how do we know if they are comprehending?

Problems With Dense Texts

School curricula, administrators, or teachers usually mandate/ believe that the complete textbook be "covered." As teachers rush through the pages and content, ELs and low-level readers are left behind. Newkirk (2010) wrote in *The Case for Slow Reading* that students never really comprehend when there are insufficient opportunities to delve deeply into text and have text-based discussions. Since it is important for all students to engage with grade-level text, the longer texts may deter reading for those who already struggle or are learning English.

A better option is to use shorter texts or to parse longer ones. As discussed in Chapter 3, to parse a text, teachers select the sections or pages from a chapter that contain all the basic information that addresses the district's standards. The fluff is left out. While planning lessons, teachers parse texts for the week's lessons, they select the vocabulary tiers, the reading comprehension skills that better suits the genre or structure, and then the consolidation activities that ensure students learn all the material selected. At first, teachers may be reluctant to cut out sections, but as their students experience more and more success, teachers became comfortable with parsing. This makes it easier for the teacher to model ways to reread, interpret, and help students internalize good reading habits.

What Does It Take to Teach Content and Reading?

A Comprehensive Approach for Student Motivation

The more exposure ELs have to explicit integrated instruction of vocabulary, reading skills, and in-depth focus on a specific domain, the more improvement on reading fluency and intrinsic motivation to learn that subject. It must become "a vibrant vicious cycle" where vocabulary, reading comprehension, and writing use the same

Discussion and ample discourse opportunities lead to deep learning.

words, but also enhance the reading and learning of more words when this cycle happens daily. Knowing the middle and high school students of today, that explicit integrated instruction also needs to have more active and interactive strategies to keep them engaged. This is why teacher talk is reduced as students take on responsibility for their own and their peers' learning. So, we are saying, "Get off the stage!" The teacher needs to turn the learning over to the students, and the students need to assume the lead instead of passively sitting in the audience. Later on, we share some classroom climate or classroom management strategies that help establish a collective efficacy environment for learning.

College and Career Readiness and Success

To build a foundation for college and career readiness, ELs must read widely and deeply from among a broad range of high-quality texts, increasingly challenging literary and informational texts. Through extensive reading of stories, dramas, poems, and myths from diverse cultures and different time periods, students gain literary and cultural knowledge as well as familiarity with various text structures and elements. By reading grade-level texts in history/social studies, science, and other disciplines, ELs build a foundation of knowledge in these fields that will also give them the background to be better readers in all content areas. All students can only gain this foundation when the curriculum is intentionally and coherently structured to develop rich content knowledge within and across grades. Students also acquire the habits of reading independently and closely, which are essential to their future success.

Understanding Close Reading

Close Reading is thoughtful, critical analysis of a text that focuses on significant details or patterns in order to develop a deep, precise understanding of the text's form, craft, meanings, etc. It is a key requirement of State Standards and directs the reader's attention to the text itself (https://nieonline.com/tbtimes/downloads/CCSS_reading.pdf).

As we have indicated in this book, one of the first steps is to find a "worthy" text for ELs to use as a Mentor Text for a variety of learning events. The text should be written in language not too difficult for the EL proficiency level, but rich enough in vocabulary, content, and ideas that can be explored across several days.

Selecting a Text for EL Close Reading

1. Vocabulary—academic and content domain language, many Tier 2 words and phrases

2. Syntax—appropriate for EL background and events and concepts logically presented

3. Text Structures—descriptive, compare-contrast, sequential, cause and effect, problem and solution

These text selection criteria are valid for any text an EL will need to read and comprehend. Any text that will be used in the general content classroom can also serve as a Mentor Text in the ESL/ELD classroom to teach strategies they will need in the regular classroom. For instance, a social studies teacher might expect students to compare and contrast points of view about the civil war applying the basic steps of close reading. In such a case, the ESL/ELD teacher can teach comparing/contrasting text features such as maps or timelines, and sentence structures, Tier 2 connectors, and take the ELs through rereading iterations to delve deeper into the main ideas, messages, and key information. The ESL/ELD teacher and the social studies teacher can agree beforehand on how to parallel close reading strategies in both lessons so as to teach closely related items, but not over-teach to the point of boredom for the ELs. The double dose of similar strategies will help ELs comprehend the social studies text, participate with more confidence throughout the learning of details and perspectives of the civil war, plus learn more English language structures and mechanics that will transfer to other curricula as well.

Beth Burke recommends steps for close reading (https://nieonline .com/tbtimes/downloads/CCSS_reading.pdf) that we have adapted for ELs and follows the ExC-ELL model.

Steps for Close Reading

1. First Read—Key Ideas and Details—Conduct Partner Reading with Summarization that focuses on ideas and details of a story or expository text elements. The teacher selects and preteaches initial vocabulary.

2. Second Read—Craft and Structure—Teacher conducts a one-paragraph Think-Aloud to model finding text features and structures, author's craft (dialogue, simile, symbolism), ideas or messages that illustrate author's purpose and craft. Subsequently, partners reread a second paragraph to search for similar text elements. The teacher selects and preteaches key terms that represent all elements, models different types of questions, and provides question starters.

3. Third Read—Integration of Knowledge and Ideas. In teams of four, students go back into the text to formulate questions around features, structures, craft, and ideas. These questions are used in a Numbered Heads Together with the whole class to discuss, synthesize, analyze, and evaluate ideas/messages. The culminating synthesis is done through a Write-Around where students draft, Ratiocinate, "Cut-n-Grow" and finalize a composition that integrates the knowledge and ideas learned, as well as the academic language that represents that topic. The teacher preteaches key terms for the Write-Around process.

Figure 4.1   Reciprocal Effects

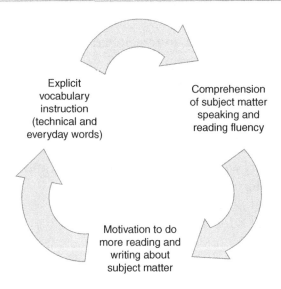

Explicit vocabulary instruction (technical and everyday words)

Comprehension of subject matter speaking and reading fluency

Motivation to do more reading and writing about subject matter

Lesson Integration Tools

Planning (Before) Students Read

To plan a lesson, teachers recommend the following for the first five components of the lesson plan (Preteaching of Vocabulary, Teacher Think-Alouds, Student Peer Reading, Peer Summaries, Depth of Word Studies/Grammar) as described in Chapter 2. Concomitantly with these, the standards, objectives, and outcomes must be selected.

Content and Language Objectives

- Select the content and language standards. This helps you to do backwards planning, where the outcome is determined first, then the lesson is designed.
- Next, the text is perused and parsed to make sure it addresses the standards, is high interest, and appropriate for reading to develop depth of comprehension and academic language for your subject.
- Once the outcomes are determined, preview the text to select key words and sentence structures, eliminate pages with unnecessary information, and parse the text for orchestrating students' daily learning tasks.

- To measure the outcomes, student assessments are selected or developed next. Map learning progressions toward those outcomes.
- Some important points to remember:
  - Translate the standards into EL English—student-friendly language (it will help all students, too).
  - Identify success criteria for your students. This is the differentiation piece. Consider the success criteria for your
    - Newcomers
    - Students with Interrupted Formal Education (SIFE)
    - Long-Term ELs
    - General EL population
    - General Education population
    - Dually Identified ELs
- Explain the standards and expectations at the beginning of the lesson, show an example while teaching/discussing, and review for completion at the end of the lesson.
- Focus on learning outcome not just an activity.
- Integrate peer interaction in as many places as possible.

Guiding Questions

Teachers use the following set of questions to plan the reading comprehension part of the lesson:

1. Vocabulary selection and instruction
   - Which Tier 1, 2, and 3 words will I teach to help my ELs understand the main aspects of the text selection?
   - What sentence frame will I use for partners to practice using the word 12 times during Step 6 of preteaching vocabulary? Can my students use the target words successfully numerous times in those 60 seconds?
   - Have I paired/grouped my learners with their levels in mind? Which activities need to be heterogeneous, and which need to be homogeneous? When was the last time I revisited these groupings? Do I have new students that may need to be placed? Have some of my students progressed enough that they need a different grouping?
   - How do I monitor to make sure that pairs interact with each word at least 12 times prior to the lesson?
   - Which words do I put on their Table Tents?
   - What do I need to model for this part of the lesson?

2. Connecting students' prior knowledge with new knowledge

- Is the text appropriate in content and complexity?
- Where do I parse the text for partner reading?
- What text features should I highlight?
- What is the main text structure? What other feature/structure do I highlight?
- What do Newcomers know about this topic? How can I find out?
- What type of motivation and realia can I use to connect to what we are about to read and learn?
- What do I need to model/script out to model for this part of the lesson?

3. Metacognitive strategies

- Which reading strategies are most appropriate for comprehending this text?
- How do I present them in my Read-Aloud/Think-Aloud? Have I scripted out and practiced this piece of modeling?
- Which is the best paragraph for the students to practice the skills I model?
- How will I debrief what they have learned after applying the strategy(ies) I modeled?

4. Active and engaged reading

- What are the best sections for partner reading and summarization?
- What type of oral summaries do I model? What type of questions do I model? What do I add to their Table Tent? Which Table Tent or supports to they need? (see www.ExC-ELL.com for examples)
- Where do we stop and debrief?
- What are my debriefing questions for the final discussion *after reading?*
- What vocabulary do I need to assess and if needed teach "on the run" while reading, and what should I revisit after reading?

5. After reading and oral summarization

- Is there a graphic or cognitive organizer they can use after reading?
- What level of Bloom's Taxonomy should they use to formulate questions?
- What follow-up cooperative learning strategies should I use to consolidate knowledge and develop more language skills?

- What mini-lessons or strategies/organizers do I need to teach before they can be successful with these skills?
- What do I need to model for this part of the lesson?
- What support and materials will they need to complete these activities?

6. Writing (see writing strategies in Chapters 7 and 8)

- What quick informal accountability strategy will I use? Exit Ticket? Journal entry? Content knowledge or language knowledge? Can I do both?
- What will they write about in their brief Exit Ticket? Can they do the Exit Ticket I have planned in one to two sentences max?
- What type of writing will they need to do for this topic?
- What Ratiocination component should I model?
- What details or evidence should they focus on for the Cut-n-Grow strategy?
- What mini-lessons for writing (paraphrasing, quoting, citing, summarizing, formulating a conclusion) do I need to teach, model, or remodel?

7. Assessments

- How should I assess their content knowledge? How do I do it at the same time as I assess their language knowledge?
- What evidence of vocabulary, grammar, critical thinking, and other skills do I want them to exhibit?
- What rubrics should I use for their writing?
- What rubrics/identification strategies should I use for their cooperative/collaborative skills while working in pairs, triads, and teams of four?
- What other types of assessments fit here?

Posting, Scaffolding, and Supporting in the Classroom

Objectives, Standards, and Expectations

States require use of core content standards and language standards. With that in mind, it is important to start developing a lesson with both standards in mind.

The standard, objective, and purpose for reading and learning and how students will be graded are posted on the chalkboard. In other words, objectives, rubrics, and evaluation criteria are posted and introduced before the lesson begins. In addition to posting in student-friendly language, introducing, revisiting throughout the lesson, and reviewing the objectives and standards at the end of each lesson help ELs and all learners see the relevance of the expectations. In addition, it shows progress and success. It also helps you as the teacher gage whether you covered them in the lesson or need to revisit them again at the beginning of the next lesson.

Content Standards, Objectives, or Expectations

Science, social studies, and state standards guide English language arts and math. Each state has its own adaptations of the standards; however, prevalent standards throughout the states focus on the following concepts. These are by no means comprehensive but are provided as examples only:

Key Ideas and Details in ELA

✓ Read closely to determine what the text says explicitly and to make logical inferences from it; cite specific textual evidence when writing or speaking to support conclusions drawn from the text.
✓ Determine central ideas, themes, or processes represented in a text and analyze their development; summarize the key supporting details and ideas.
✓ Analyze how and why individuals, events, formulas, or ideas develop and interact over the course of a text.

Key Ideas and Details in Science

✓ Cite specific textual evidence to support analysis of science and technical texts.
✓ Determine the central ideas or conclusions of a text; provide an accurate summary of the text distinct from prior knowledge or opinions.
✓ Follow precisely a multistep procedure when carrying out experiments, taking measurements, or performing technical tasks.

Key Ideas and Details in Social Studies

✓ Cite specific textual evidence to support analysis of primary and secondary sources.
✓ Determine the central ideas or information of a primary or secondary source; provide an accurate summary of the source distinct from prior knowledge or opinions.

✓ Identify key steps in a text's description of a process related to history/social studies (e.g., how a bill becomes law, how interest rates are raised or lowered).

Key Ideas and Details in Math

✓ Summarize, represent, and interpret data.
✓ Justify why a mathematical statement is true or false.
✓ Create equations that describe number or relationships.

Craft and Structure

The craft and structure, integration of knowledge and ideas, and reading complexity are part of all subjects. While all craft and structure are related and transferable across curricula, each of these subject matters have specific standards for expressing and measuring their own standard. The standards we show as examples below are ELA-based but are applicable for the other subjects. As you read them, consider which subjects they may be related to and the specificity needed to be successful in each.

✓ Interpret words and phrases as they are used in a text, including determining technical, connotative, and figurative meanings, and analyze how specific word choices shape meaning or tone.
✓ Analyze the structure of texts, including how specific sentences, paragraphs, and larger portions of the text (e.g., a section, chapter, scene, or stanza) relate to each other and the whole.
✓ Assess how point of view or purpose shapes the content and style of a text.

Integration of Knowledge and Ideas

✓ Integrate and evaluate content presented in diverse media and formats, including visually and quantitatively, as well as in words.[1]
✓ Delineate and evaluate the argument and specific claims in a text, including the validity of the reasoning as well as the relevance and sufficiency of the evidence.
✓ Analyze how two or more texts address similar themes or topics to build knowledge or to compare the approaches the authors take.

Range of Reading and Level of Text Complexity

* Read and comprehend complex literary and informational texts independently and proficiently.

What to Post

Even highly educated adults and educators need assistance in unpacking the standards. As mentioned above, all standards and expectations should be posted, reviewed, and discussed in student-friendly terms. Posting the litany of numbers such as EEn.2.6.3&4 does nothing to help the students. Copying EEn.2.6.3&4 word for word on the board or having students copy it is equally useless and ineffective, even for non-EL students. Here it is as written in the standards guide: "EEn.2.6.3 Analyze the impacts that human activities have on global climate change. EEn.2.6.4 Attribute changes to Earth's systems to global climate change." Now add the related standards for seventh-grade writing (WS7.9.b). "Draw evidence from … informational texts to support analysis, reflection, and research. b. Apply grade 7 Reading standards to literary nonfiction." Did you notice that the standard also refers to Grade 7 Reading standards?

Rather, if the students are about to read a text(s) about climate change, these friendlier objectives and expectations might be what a teacher posts (and discusses and reviews):

Content Objectives (examples)

✓ You will identify statements or claims about climate change made by the author.
✓ You will determine and explain what evidence the author used to support these statements or claims.
✓ You will identify any counterclaims mentioned and explain why they were refuted.
✓ You will describe cause-and-effect relationships explained by the author.

Language Objectives (examples)

✓ Vocabulary: You will use Tier 1, 2, and 3 vocabulary from our text/s sufficiently for reading, writing, speaking, and listening.
✓ Reading: You will determine the main idea and provide an objective summary of the text. Make sure to identify and justify the claims made by the author.

✓ Listening and Speaking: Engage in a range of collaborative discussions in a variety of teams and partnerships.

✓ Writing: Engage in a Write-Around to draft, edit, and revise the article about climate change.

For Assessment (examples)

✓ You will need to write a paragraph each day until we finish the unit.

✓ In each paragraph, you will need to explain what we have learned about how the Earth's climate is changing and what the U.S. Environmental Agencies report as the major causes of climate change.

✓ Be sure to use Tier 2 and Tier 3 words from the article we are reading.

✓ Remember to include transitions/connectors, signal words, and combinations of independent and dependent clauses in your sentences.

ELs may still need explicit instruction in many of the words used in the "student-friendly" versions, depending upon their ESL/ELD level; however, the discussion of these words will also help them to be successful and feel as if they have accomplished the goal for the lesson. Which of the above would you as the learner find easier to accomplish?

In place of a word wall or only Tier 3 words on bulletin boards, lists of Tier 1, 2, and 3 words on chart paper or laminated charts are posted. These are taken down when a new lesson is presented and new words need to be learned. See Figure 4.2 for an example we saw a math teacher use to post her Tiered Vocabulary during the Winter Olympics: Bronze—Tier 1, Silver—Tier 2, Gold—Tier 3.

Figure 4.2   Tier 1, 2, and 3 Words

Bronze	Silver	Gold
• then	• simplify	• fractions
• last	• equivalent	• ratios
• next	• reduce	• lowest terms
• first	• compare	• denominator
• on top	• ascending	• Integer
• underneath	• decending	• mixed numbers
	• describe	• numerator
	• relationship	• extend and divide

Table Tents

First, I said, . . .
Then, she replied, . . .
After that, Henry explained, . . .
Lastly, Koichi screamed, . . .
Thus, Elvira exclaimed, . . .
Finally, the teacher declared, . . .

They stated, . . .
Julio whispered, . . .
Arika mumbled, . . .
Maggie muttered, . . .
Yesenia yelled, . . .

COLD
cool, frosty, chilly, freezing, icy, frozen, wintery

HOT
fiery, boiling, red-hot, heated, scorching, sizzling, scalding, warm, burning, ablaze, baking

Five Paragraph Essay

Paragraph 1   Hook
Thesis Statement

Paragraph 2   Topic Sentence
Evidence
Explanation

Paragraph 3   Topic Sentence
Evidence
Explanation

Paragraph 4   Topic Sentence
Evidence
Explanation

Paragraph 5 Reworded Thesis
Summary

RUN
sprint
race

lope
dart

dash
jog

gallop
scamper

GOOD
exceptional magnificent
remarkable meaningful
superb outstanding
exemplar superior

BAD
useless unpleasant
unimportant dreadful
horrendous inconsequential
irrational
pathetic illogical
harmful

© 2016 Margarita Calderón & Associates

Some useful Tier 2 words such as those in Chapter 3 should be included in table tents for continuous use. They tend to look like tents or tents on their side. One teacher typed them on an index card and laminated them. The students would carry them from class to class in their pockets or back packs.

For Specific Reading Strategies

A variety of posters can also become Table Tents. Have different ones for close reading, another for writing a lab report, and others for class discussions where Accountable Talk or Responsible Discourse is desired or as sentence starters for those who need help starting a sentence, but know the answer.

Classroom Posters

Accountable Talk: Agreement	Accountable Talk: Disagreement
I agree . . .	I disagree . . .
I agree, however, I would like to add . . .	I respectfully disagree . . .
	I disagree due to . . .
I want to echo . . .	However, the author states, . . .
I concur . . .	
	On the other hand, . . .
Moreover, . . .	However, in the text, . . .
Furthermore, . . .	
Based on . . ., I . . .	
In addition, . . .	

Cooperative Learning social norms are important to post and review occasionally. The norms are selected according to behaviors teachers deem as necessary after observing students work in teams. Some of those norms could be:

- Respect one another.
- Contribute ideas.
- Accept ideas.
- Politely disagree and show evidence.

The ExC-ELL Reading Sequence Before Reading

Teacher Read-Aloud/Think-Aloud in Content Classes

After five or six vocabulary words/phrases are pretaught, *the teacher reads a short paragraph to model reading comprehension strategies.* In secondary schools, teachers Read-Aloud to model reading strategies, fluency, and comprehension skills—*not to read to the students.* There is a strong mistaken belief that because students have trouble reading, it is better for the teacher to read to the students. We emphasize the inaccuracy of this because we have observed teachers read complete novels to their classes! Keeping students from reading only makes them fall further and further behind on their reading skills.

For the Teacher Read-Aloud/Think-Aloud process, the teacher starts with *one* of the statements below and then proceeds to model how the process is done.

- I'm going to visualize and think aloud about what we are going to read.
- I'm going to read chunks I can handle and then stop and summarize.
- I'm going to call the title and subheadings text features and find other features.
- I'm going to make predictions.

Next, as the teacher explains or reminds students that he or she is "thinking-aloud" as a student and is modeling the Think-Aloud process, he or she will add the following highlights as appropriate.

- What could that word mean? Let me reread.
- I'm going to stop and reread confusing parts of this sentence.
- I'm going to put a Post-It note after this sentence so I can ask for clarification.
- What kind of test question would the teacher ask from this paragraph?
- How does this relate to the paragraph above?

Teacher Read-Aloud

Think-Aloud becomes a teacher Read-Aloud and will need to be practiced and intentionally scripted, planned, and practiced as part of the lesson planning stage. This metacognitive process is automatic, almost instinctive for most adults and virtually impossible to do with clarity and specificity of purpose. Thus, scripting and practicing the script to pointedly highlight the concept you want to feature helps with clarity of purpose. As part of this strategy, students practice Think-Aloud using the concept just modeled when they first are introduced to the process and then each time a new concept is highlighted while the teacher circulates throughout the class monitoring for success and understanding.

Read-Aloud is not limited to word or text comprehension. Teachers should use this strategy to point out text features, text structures, grammar, and mechanics, or even those content, language, and assessment expectations. The following are categories of concepts and mechanics that are perfect and necessary for Think-Alouds.

Text Features

In expository or nonfiction writing, text features are those elements that serve as road signs. Text features help the reader comprehend what they are reading and are building blocks for text structures (text structures are explained below). Think-Aloud can be used to explain different text features such as those that appear in glossaries, newspapers, tables of contents, and pictures, captions, and side bars in science and social studies texts. Students can point to and touch text features and then think aloud how they help them to understand what they are reading. Fiction or literary texts use these features and those better known as story elements: characters, setting, plot, theme, etc., or physical shapes of narrative such as different types of poetry.

More to Think About for Think-Alouds

There are other basic reading (decoding) and reading comprehension skills that can be modeled and taught while doing a teacher Read-Aloud such as identifying prefixes, suffixes, and root words; a compound sentence; an incomplete sentence. We can also call these text features because they are things we can touch as we spot them. Some of the ones ELs, especially Newcomers and even low-level readers, need the most in secondary content classes are listed here along with ways teachers can teach them as mini-lessons "on the run" without having to stop and conduct a grammar or phonics lesson with separate materials. *Grammar and phonics make more sense to the students when examples come from the texts they are currently reading.*

Grammar, Spelling, Phonics, and Comprehension Skills to Highlight During Teacher Read-Alouds

1. *Auditory Blending and Segmenting.* With a difficult word, blend sounds for 2-, 3-, or 4-phoneme words or break a word into its separate sounds.

2. *Sight Words.* Mention and read words in context, especially those that have irregular spelling or pronunciation.

3. *Vocabulary.* Say the word, have students repeat it three times, and follow it with a simple definition or a simple example. Have students reread aloud the sentence the word is from.

4. *Cognate Awareness.* Recognize cognates and false cognates in the passage.

5. *Spelling.* Say the word, then spell the word aloud as you are reading.

6. *Writing Mechanics.* Mention or emphasize punctuation, sentence structures, grammar, idioms, and metaphors.

7. *Fluency.* Read a sentence without fluency (too slow, too fast, wrong pauses, wrong intonation), then read it again with smoothness, good expression, good rate.

8. *Comprehension Monitoring.* Model comprehension monitoring and "fix-it" strategies. Make a mistake in reading, and then go back and fix it.

9. *Predictions.* After reading part of a paragraph, make a prediction.

10. *Questions.* Ask a question after you read a couple of lines.

11. *Answer Questions.* After you ask a question, model answering that question in complete sentences.

12. *Contrastive Linguistics: Grammar.* Talk about specific sentence structures, tense, punctuation, and contrastive features of Spanish and English or English and another language when possible.

13. *Word Analysis.* Mention prefixes, suffixes, identifying word parts, and deconstruct and construct compound words.

14. *Summarization.* Read a couple of sentences, then summarize aloud.

15. *Text structures:* Read a paragraph and then find either the main idea, details, cause and effect, problem-solution, evidence finding, etc.

16. *Text Related Writing.* Before students begin a writing assignment, think aloud how you would tackle prewriting, writing, revising, editing, publishing, using vocabulary and patterns from the text you have been reading.

We don't want the students overwhelmed; therefore, only one or two of the strategies above should be modeled at one time. After modeling one or two strategies, instruct the students to use those as they conduct their partner reading.

Text Analysis and Cognitive Strategies

Structure	Tier 2 Words
• Description • Provides a specific topic and its attributes • Main idea(s) is/are supported by rich/descriptive details	above, across, all, also, appears to be, as an example, behind, below, beside, by observing, characteristics are, for example, for instance
• Sequence • Provides information/events in chronological order • Details are in specific order to convey specific meaning	additionally, after, after that, afterward, another, at __ (time), before, during, finally, first, following, initially, last, later, meanwhile, next
• Problem/Solution • Problems are identified and solutions are provided • Supporting details describe the problem and solution	accordingly, answer, as a result, because, challenge, decide, fortunately, if __ then, issue, one reason is, outcome is, problem, so
• Cause/Effect • Tells an event or action and the reason(s) it happened • Cause = what happened, why it happened • Effect = what happened as a result, the impact is/was	accordingly, as a result, because, because of, consequently, due to, effects of, for this/that reason, if, if ___ then, in order to, is caused by, lead/s to, since, so, so that, thereby, therefore, this led to, thus, when ____ the, responsible for
• Compare/Contrast • Gives the similarities and differences of 2 or more items/ideas/objects/places • Examines how things are alike or different	also, although, as opposed to, as well as, both, but, compared to/with, different, different from, either ____ or, however, in comparison, in contrast, instead of, like, likewise, on the other hand, resembles, same/same as, similar(ly), too, unlike, while, yet

The understanding of all classroom texts in secondary schools is crucial. To delve deeply into comprehension, students need to have a command of cognitive strategies for identifying main idea/central idea and important details, identifying cause and effect, knowing how to compare or contrast, follow a multistep procedure when carrying out experiments, and so on. For this, ELs will need the tools of

Text Features	
• Title	• Labels
• Table of contents	• Text boxes
• Index	• Maps
• Glossary	• Charts
• Heading	• Hyperlinks
• Keywords	• Icons
• Illustrations and photographs	• Bullets
• Sidebars	• Timelines
• Captions	• Cutaways
• Diagrams	• Graphs
	• Text types

appropriate discourse. Sentence starters or frames on their Table Tents can include:

I agree because on page ….

I disagree because on page ….

I agree; however, I would like to add ….

I believe the cause is on page ….

I concur ….

Moreover, ….

Furthermore, ….

Based on … I ….

In addition, ….

What would happen if …?

Can you say more about …?

Teaching Text Structures

Fiction and nonfiction authors use text structures to explain craft and structure: the author's purpose and craft. Authors use these text structures: cause and effect, problem/solution, persuasive, argumentative, descriptive, sequential, compare and contrast. These structures can also be explained by selecting a passage that illustrates it and doing a Think-Aloud, and asking students to find similar passages as they read. Students also need to make connections with other texts or ideas for their own lives. The more a teacher models and displays language structures and connectors, the better the outcomes during discussions and in writing assignments.

Teachers also like to post in their rooms charts such as the following, which contains the text structures and the Tier 2 words that authors typically use and that the ELs can use for discussions and writing.

Strategy Process Notes: Metacognitive Think-Alouds, Text Features, and Structure

For the Think-Aloud strategy, it is imperative that until you are proficient in doing this strategy aloud, you will need to script out what you want to say and practice it aloud. The adult brain automatically processes much of what you as the teacher want to explicitly show in a Think-Aloud, and therefore practicing aloud with your script will seem strange at first but will help with the clarity of what you are trying to highlight. Also, for this strategy, 1 or 2 minutes and one or two concepts is sufficient, or the students and the purpose are lost. If you have several concepts or items you want to highlight from a Mentor Text or for a lesson, do separate Think-Alouds to feature what you want the students to master.

And as always, debrief with your students. Tell them upfront that you will be doing a Think-Aloud and then ask them how this helps them understand the text, expectation, or lesson. Remind them to pay attention as you may ask them to do a Think-Aloud later. When we discuss Partner Reading, student Think-Alouds are one of the variations of Partner Reading used to focus for increased comprehension.

In Chapter 5, we continue with content consolidation strategies for cooperative learning, classroom debriefing, and student discourse.

Summary

✓ All middle and high school teachers are reading teachers.

✓ Whole-school implementation accelerates everyone's reading skills; core content or electives.

✓ Conversation with whole faculty dispels obstructing myths.

✓ Student interaction is key to reading.

✓ There are basic lesson integration tools.

✓ All teachers must address language, literacy, and content standards.

✓ Tools for students are a must.

✓ There is an evidenced-based sequence for teachers to use before students approach the text to read.

✓ Reading content rich and descriptive text is discussed in Chapter 5.

5

Content Reading

Conclusion 8-8: There is less research on effective instructional practices for high school ELs than for the other grade spans. However, some promising practices include a focus on academic language development that embraces all facets of academic language and includes both oral and written language across content areas; structured reading and writing instruction using a cognitive strategies approach and explicit instruction in reading comprehension strategies; opportunities for extended discussion of text and its meaning between teachers and students and in peer groups that may foster motivation and engagement in literacy learning; provision of peer-assisted learning opportunities; and rigorous, focused, and relevant support for long-term ELs.

—National Academies of Sciences, Engineering, and Medicine (NAS; 2017)

Every Student Succeeds Act and What It Means for Content Teachers

The Every Student Succeeds Act (ESSA) sets out to hold schools and states accountable for making sure every student does learn content and succeeds.

States need to hold schools accountable for helping English language learners become proficient. . . . Schools need to come up with a 'research-based' maximum timeline for ELs to become proficient in English. The idea is to encourage schools to make sufficient progress each year in helping ELs master their new language. (Klein, 2016)

Mastering English involves more than attending an ESL/ELD class, a class that for many students is at best an hour a day—frequently less. Since we know where our ELs are the rest of the day, that puts the onus of ESSA on the content teacher as well. Since we know that one ESL/ELD teacher or only the ESL/ELD teachers in a school cannot accomplish all the language and literacy skills required for students to succeed in the disciplines, the proper thing to do to keep the whole school afloat is to provide professional development for the whole school as quickly as possible. Using the whole-school approach means less work for all participants. *In previous chapters, we have discussed and outlined many of the facets of planning, preteaching what supports the actual reading of the text.* Content text specificity is also required so that every student succeeds in comprehending the *dense grade-level texts they will be reading.*

In this chapter, we add more information and instructional strategies researched and found effective in helping ELs to dive into reading and emerge at the end of the text as successful readers. We begin by discussing the different structural makeup of each subject and its individual language. We will feature Partner Reading and Summation and student-centered Reciprocal Teaching. We will also highlight those times and areas where vocabulary instruction needs to occur while students are reading, and how to integrate and monitor the metacognitive strategies we just discussed in Chapter 4.

Literature

For example, most ELs are taught to read with narrative/literature texts. Literature (e.g., short stories, fables, children's stories, poetry, British vs. English classics) contains idioms, metaphors, symbolism, theme, allusion, and word play that make this difficult for ELs to learn both literary content and English as an additional language. Although many words in short stories are short (Tier 1: See Chapter 3), many have multiple meanings. Some are false cognates and deceive the reader into thinking they comprehend. Literature text consists of short stories, poems, and novels that vary in both features and structures. Moreover, the vocabulary, grammatical features, and purpose of literature vary considerably from that of science, social studies, and math. Literature uses metaphor, symbolism, theme, allusion, foreshadowing, and similar concepts to understand with depth. English language arts teachers need to be more explicit about explaining and modeling what *metaphor, symbolism, theme, allusion,* and *foreshadowing* look like and where an example appears in the text the students are about to read. Getting through text features and structures is only the first long step for ELs. The most difficult part comes when it is time to interpret the literature. Without explicit instruction on all the terminology involved, they are left in the dark.

Of course, the other challenge for teachers is the students' limited background knowledge of U.S. literature. For the most part, Newcomers will not have read the typical elementary trade books (e.g., *Charlotte's Web, Alexander's Terrible* ...) and will not be familiar with broad categories of genre (e.g., short story, novel, poetry, drama, folk stories, chants, science fiction, fable, myth, mystery). Worse yet, even Long-Term ELs probably missed out on direct instruction on how to read a range of literary texts. They might have been asked about the symbolism in their texts, but no one modeled for them how to detect symbolism, figurative language, and how to make inferences from other rhetorical tools (e.g., irony, satire, problems of point of view). Even the settings may be unfamiliar (e.g., Paris, Greece). Thus, a quick overview through Teacher Think-Alouds is the next step after teaching key words.

Without these cultural and literary references, how can ELs make intertextual links, allusions to other texts, character types, or tragic heroes? The challenge for language arts teachers is to learn how to help ELs and other striving readers to develop conceptual understanding, while concurrently learning the complex language of literature and how to read that complex language. A Carnegie report reminds us that "Reading deeply complex literary texts offers unique opportunities for students to wrestle with some of the core ethical dilemmas that we face as human beings" (Lee & Spratley, 2010). For Margarita, as an English Learner in high school, literature was her gate into understanding and fitting into the U.S. culture and human nature, thanks to her English teacher.

Science

We believe that science could be a better vehicle for ELs to learn English. Science has fewer verbs and more nouns. There are pictures, graphs, and tables to increase precision of information. Teachers can increase comprehension by pointing out the purpose of text features such as abstracts, section headings, figures, tables, diagrams, maps, drawings, photographs, reference lists, and endnotes, during a teacher Think-Aloud. However, science texts also often require mathematical literacy to understand what mathematical tables and figures convey. When this additional crossover to math occurs, a Think-Aloud is the perfect way to highlight such a shift in the text.

Science writing has attributive adjectives and prepositional phrases that can be taught together as one-word Tier 3 phrases (For more about Tier 3 and the other tiers, see Chapter 3). For example: *heat-trapping gases, global average temperature, record of increased global atmospheric*, etc. Science also uses Tier 2 connectors such as *therefore, nevertheless, over the course of,* and *notwithstanding*—words that are often found in state exams. Although obvious to some readers, it is also helpful to point out that syntax in scientific texts may define complex technical terms within a sentence (e.g., an invisible gas called vapor; animals that eat plants, herbivores, may be found). Frequently scientific texts contain structure vocabulary such as *if ___ then, the outcome is, one reason, since, as opposed to, compared to, different from*, etc. The technical vocabulary or Tier 3 words most often have Latin or Greek roots. Fortunately, that means that science also has a copious word bank of cognates (e.g., dermatology = *dermatología* or *dermatologie*; cosmos = *cosmos* [Spanish] and *cosmos* [French]). Science is also very hands-on, and with explicit instruction on vocabulary before lab work, students can proceed with the appropriate safety and cognitive understanding. However, the tasks of observing, thinking, experimenting, and validating will require close reading processes where ELs can revisit the text and interact with peers as they interact with experiments and scientific processes.

Social Studies

Social studies texts include language from history, political science, sociology, and economics. Primary source texts (newspapers, books, pamphlets, cartoons, laws, diaries, letters, paintings, photographs, presidential speeches) also have their own vocabulary, structures, and purpose. These also reflect the author's point of view. Students read history to understand and interpret various historical events, documents, and processes. Students read contemporary documents, including newspapers, to learn to reason about political issues.

Social studies texts typically contain long sentences with several propositions (e.g., it, them, they, which), making reading difficult to decipher. This will require navigating techniques for ELs and other readers. Prior knowledge will probably be the greatest difficulty for ELs. Whereas many non-ELs were exposed to bit and pieces about the Boston Tea Party throughout their elementary grades, Newcomers will have no clue as to what kind of party the Bostonians held.

History is not just a series of facts to memorize, but rather a series of competing interpretive narratives. Teachers must instruct students on how to compare, and use procedures for analyzing contradictory sources, determining reliability and argument to the best explanation. We will touch on argumentative discourse later in this chapter. Social studies and science also call for developing the skill of "sourcing"— that is evaluating and weighing evidence by considering its source. Students need to ask themselves, "Who wrote this and why?" "For what audience?" "What was the author's purpose?" "How do I know this source is reliable?"

In addition to specialized vocabulary such as *Declaration of Independence, Emancipation Proclamation, henceforth, powerful,* and *human capital,* history texts regularly use features—pictures, timelines, sequences of events, and maps—to provide background knowledge and set the tone for reading. If students need to pay attention to sourcing, they will have to know the source and reliability of that source, the author's purpose, and the intended audience.

Math

Counterintuitive to logic, even in today's education arena, there is still the belief that "There's no reading in math." In fact, considering current state standards, there is a phenomenal amount of reading in math and even more need for students to learn to use language to read and work through problems. They must understand and then communicate ideas coherently and clearly to organize ideas and structure arguments. There is specialized language that needs to be introduced such as the example in Chapter 3 for the word *translation.* Even the simple process of addition is not just simply conveyed with the word *add.* For example, consider the short word problem that follows. "Lupita had three apples and found two more. How many does she have now?" When written numerically, it is easy $(3 + 2 = ?)$, but what words mean + and what words mean = ? Teachers use at least four or five different ways to talk about "adding" during a lesson: *add, all together, together, combine, how many in all, join, plus, sum, what does that make.* Can you imagine an EL trying to figure out the instructions for a simple addition? The word *similar* is another word that stumps ELs. Similar means alike in other subjects, but in math, rectangles are *similar* only if the ratio of the short sides equals the ratio of the long sides.

Students may know how to do math, but often they don't understand what the question is asking. In addition to the unique page formatting and structure of most mathematics texts, the basic structure of mathematics problems differs from that of most informational text. In a traditional reading paragraph, there is a topic sentence at the beginning, and the remaining sentences fill in details that expand on and support this main idea; in a mathematics problem, the key idea often comes at the end of the paragraph in the form of a question. Students must learn to read the problem to ascertain the main idea and then read it again to figure out which details and numbers relate to the question being posed and which are redundant. Students must visualize the problem's context, and then apply strategies that they think will lead to a solution, using the appropriate data from the problem statement (Kenney, Hancewicz, Heuer, Metsisto, & Tuttle, 2005).

However, math learning also implies generic reading strategies such as previewing, making predictions, rereading, and summarizing. Students are expected to write the logic of proofs in a paragraph form that includes words as well as mathematical notation. Then, they are expected to produce such problems/texts themselves. To accomplish such tasks, ELs need explicit and repeated instruction on the specific Tier 1, 2, and 3 vocabulary, syntactic structures, and the form of communication that mathematics uses and will be found in the SAT and ACT and new state exams. For example, reading practices can focus on reading to get meaning, to extract specific information, to find an example of something, to generate a reflective written response, or to make sense of graphic or visual text.

Computers, Dance, Band, Art, and All Other Enrichment Courses

Many times, these are the courses that anchor a student in their new culture. Most of these have standards that must be achieved. ELs not only are entitled to take these classes, but should be encouraged to do so as well. Consider a Driver's Education class. How much academic language and comprehension is required to take a driver's license test, understand the responsibility of having insurance, and use the correct language, discourse register, and vocabulary with the police officer who may have pulled you over for a traffic infraction? Business and Technology curricula? Fine Arts? Do not each have their own specific language, structure, and syntax? As an elective or enrichment content teacher, you too are part of the whole-school implementation process and are equally responsible for the success of your students.

Teachers are uniquely positioned to ensure content knowledge for ELs. The struggles with content standards are on the shoulders of all teachers. Therefore, these extraordinary teachers can benefit hugely from a systematic approach to professional development and collective efficacy opportunities at their schools. Chapter 9 will elaborate on some of the ways successful schools are supporting their teachers.

Too Much Sheltering in Textbooks for ELs

We find many textbook and curriculum adoptions also include sheltered content and products for ELs. Publishers of sheltered instruction or content-based ESL/ELD textbooks use readability formulas that keep ELs reading below second- or third-grade levels even in secondary schools. Important topics and concepts are reduced to a couple of sentences, devoid of detail and content that can be analyzed to practice critical thinking strategies. We have observed teachers using such sheltered content, sending, out of desperation for lack of detail, students to search in encyclopedias. The students have no recourse but to copy straight out of the pages without understanding the basic concepts and failing to be successful with end-of-year tests and standards.

Of course, there are uses at times for these supplemental materials. Newcomers, for example, at English proficiency Levels 0 or 1 can begin with simpler texts that teach both content concepts and language. However, they should quickly progress within 6 to 12 weeks through various reading levels. Newcomer Centers can select the type of initial ESL(ELD)/sheltered ELA, math, science, and social studies that enable these learning progressions in a systematic and expeditious fashion.

Partner Reading

The strategy of Partner Reading is highly and intentionally structured. After switching back and forth reading sentence by sentence to read a paragraph, students stop and summarize using as many Tier 2 and Tier 3 words as possible. They can also practice the strategy the teacher has highlighted in his Think-Aloud (e.g., finding evidence, supporting author's point, showing cause and effect, using evidence from the text).

For the base strategy of Partner Reading, structure, modeling, and classroom management are imperative. Notice the bookmark example

Figure 5.1   Partner
                   Reading

PARTNER READING

Who is Partner A?

Who is Partner B?

Partner A:
Read aloud a
sentence in
Level 1 voice.

Partner B:
Read along silently.

SWITCH

Partner B:

Read aloud a
sentence in
Level 1 voice.

Partner A:

Read along silently.

At the end of the
paragraph, Partner A
and B summarize in
Level 1 voices, with
T2 and T3
vocabulary.

we have provided in Figure 5.1. The instructions give the flow of back and forth and the reminder to summarize at the paragraph. The teacher we borrowed this example from had taught her students the editing notation of the pilcrow sign (the paragraph return symbol ¶) as a visual reminder of the end of the paragraph. Additionally, the instructions say to read aloud in "Level 1" voices. For this teacher and classroom, Level 1 voice was very, very, very low and quiet so that only reading partners could hear each other. This of course also involves having well-established classroom norms and good behavior management.

As with all new concept learning, specific instructions and modeling are needed. Especially so for ELs. Providing a written set of instructions, student-friendly explanation in writing and orally, plus modeling the new expected outcome are required. Providing students with a classroom poster of the process, Table Tents or even the bookmark give them this visual queue. Modeling the strategy for your students and discussing the process helps provide that oral scaffolding they need. Intentionally point out the process on the visuals you provide for each step. Repetition at this early stage will help later with smoother implementation. Have students summarize the instructions with a review strategy such as Turn to Your Partner (TTYP). We have seen several other memory aides such as quickly highlighting alternating sentences and starring the paragraphs to help students remember to do every other sentence and stop at the paragraph. For the initial implementation, it will take a little longer to help students work through and process the strategy. This is normal when learning a new process. It is important to not let the reminders, highlighting, etc., take too much time, and thus take away from the actual reading time. Fortunately, these help all students.

Next, model the strategy with a student or your co-teacher with whom you have already practiced the strategy. Here is how the modeling should look. Select who is Partner A and who is Partner B. Both partners are actively reading, but only one is reading aloud (in a *low* voice) at a time. Partner A starts with the first sentence and stops at the punctuation. Partner B is silently reading along with Partner A. Switching, Partner B then continues with the next sentence and stops at the punctuation. Partner A is silently reading along with Partner B. Partner A then continues with the next sentence, then Partner B, Partner A, and on until the paragraph is completed. Notice, the partner not reading in a low voice is silently reading along. At the end of the paragraph, the partners put their heads together and summarize what they have just read using Tier 2 and Tier 3 words, some of which you may have just pretaught. When modeling, remember to do the Partner Summarizing as well. Point out that for summarizing in this strategy, there is no writing. Ask for clarifying questions or a TTYP summary of what you and your partner just modeled.

The first time you introduce partner reading, and throughout the year at different intervals, it is good to revisit the steps of the strategy. One teacher we observed has the practice of remodeling each strategy when she receives a new student, EL or otherwise. In addition, we suggest that anytime you modify, use a variation, or have a different expected outcome, modeling is necessary for clarity. For modeling, choosing a student ahead of time and practicing once helps. Scripting out the steps for you and your assistant will help you to make sure that you have included all the steps and are conveying them in the manner you planned.

Now, have students practice a paragraph. Circulate among the students to check for understanding of the process. When students have completed the paragraph, debrief with them. Ask what the steps for Partner Reading are. Ask what did they get from reading this way? What did they have to do? How does this strategy help them to read better? Revisit the instructions again as needed for back and forth reading and perhaps volume.

Basic Partner Reading and Summarizing can be scheduled for 10–12 minutes. There is no writing during Partner Reading and Summarizing. This is an oral activity. There will be time for written summaries later. While students are reading, the teacher circulates the room, monitors, and collects data on comprehension, classroom interaction, possible words that need to be taught "on-the-run" or words that can be revisited.

After Partner Reading, the lesson moves on to content consolidation or post-reading vocabulary word study or segue to the next vocabulary to preteach from the next portion of parsed text. (See our website www.ExC-ELL.com for examples of Block Schedules or other lesson timeframes.)

After several weeks of alternating sentences, partners can move to alternating paragraphs, if they continue to be engaged in quality reading and quality interaction during their summarization. There are several variations, which can be used after the basic strategy is well established.

Partner Reading and Summarizing With Newcomers

Pairing an EL or a Newcomer EL with a mainstream student is beneficial for both. It helps the EL, particularly a Newcomer, to have a buddy who can help understand what reading and classroom routines are like in this country. Partnering two ELs or an EL with a Newcomer works well also. Mainstream students report they learn a lot more from helping others than they do on their own. Students have told us that they are more cautious about how they read (their fluency), and pay closer attention to what they read, and are able to understand it better because they get to talk through what they just read. Hearing questions from someone who needs explanations for basic word meanings, cultural nuances, and concept formation helps the peer tutor as much as the EL.

Many students will come during the year and need to fit into academic learning as quickly as possible. Some Newcomers can do that very well since they have high literacy levels in their own language and are highly educated already in the content. Others may need more time, even to figure out what schooling norms require from them.

For those classrooms where one or two Newcomers matriculate into the classroom, placing the student with an established EL-mainstream partnership works well. When it is time for Partner Reading, the Newcomer sits between the two students and at first listens to each of them read. We refer to this as a *Newcomer Triad*. After a week or so of listening and observing reading routines and classroom norms, the Newcomer begins to feel more comfortable. The next step is to ask the Newcomer to shadow read (read after each partner but in a soft voice), or read along with each partner softly. It helps if the Newcomer's partners use a finger or pointer to point out the words as they read. The workflow of this triad is as follows: Partner A reads a sentence, Newcomer shadow reads/repeats as much as possible the same sentence. Partner B reads the next sentence, while the Newcomer shadow reads. This continues until the end of the paragraph.

The third step is to ask the Newcomer to take turns reading on her own, but still sits between both partners. This way, the Newcomer in the middle gets more turns at reading because students are still alternating sentences, but the one in the middle gets to read twice as much. (Partner A reads, Newcomer reads her *own* sentence, Partner B reads, Newcomer reads, Partner A reads, Newcomer reads ...) This, too, continues until the end of the paragraph and on into the Summarizing. Newcomers also summarize at the end of the paragraph. If at the beginning all they accomplish is to repeat what is said, this is acceptable. Later, they will be able to summarize on their own. This Newcomer Triad scaffolding helps the student track the sounds and letters with the cadence and intonation of the punctuation and pauses needed when reading English quickly.

As a side note, this triad setup works well for any low level, striving reader or beginner learner that needs extra assistance. If an ESL/ELD teacher works with this student some time during the day, that teacher can accelerate vocabulary and reinforce concepts the student has read in the content classes. In the meantime, the mainstream teacher is applying all the steps described throughout this chapter so that there is redundancy of vocabulary usage through the lesson sequence. In the end, the triad has accomplished its task, and the Newcomer starts working with his or her own partner and the expectation of immediately participating in class is firmly established.

At times, there are Newcomer or SIFE Centers where whole classes are Newcomers. Partner Reading is still effective with a slight modification. The teacher is Partner A and reads the sentence. The very new or low-level student is the student that seats between the teacher and another EL. The new student repeats what the teacher just read. The other EL student who is near to exiting from the Newcomer Center/Program is Partner B and reads (if needed with help from the teacher) the next sentence, the others repeat, and continue to the end of the paragraph. Summarizing is included at the end of the paragraph and again if it involves the Newcomer simply repeating the summary, that too helps the student.

Strategy Process Notes: Partner Reading and Summarizing

As we discussed in Chapter 4, a large part of pre-planning a lesson is to think about the section of text to which you want students to read and respond. This is accomplished by parsing and analyzing that piece of text. It involves selecting the five words or phrases to preteach, scripting the 7 Steps of preteaching vocabulary for each of those words and phrases, selecting a feature or structure to highlight in your teacher Think-Aloud, thinking about the piece of Mentor Text you want students to read.

Next comes thinking about your intentional pairing of your students. Careful consideration should also be given to which students will be paired together or which students shouldn't be paired together. For some activities, it is fine to let them pair themselves. For Partner Reading, however, consider their primary language, ELD level, and any other factors that are pertinent to good participation and ease of learning. You may also need to consider the makeup and configuration of your room for an easy transition to the Partner Reading strategy.

Reading partners should be sitting next to each other, as in side-by-side so that both can see the single copy of the text. We suggest only one copy of the text since this both cuts down on paper if they are copied, subliminally requiring them to sit closer, and implies that this is a joint activity. Additionally, ear-to-ear reading also works. Students sit next to each other, one facing front and the other facing back: ear-to-ear. Their ear-to-ear reading gets them more engaged as they read in low voices.

Setting the Stage

After making your choices, explaining why they are being paired and seated thusly, give the instructions for Partner Reading and Summarizing. After the teacher models reading and thinking about reading, partners are assigned the parsed piece of text to read. During the first month or two of partner reading, alternating sentences helps students ease into this type of reading. Partner Reading ensures that partners are paying attention to each other and helps them concentrate on stress and juncture, punctuation (where and how to pause), in other words to read with expression or prosody. This form of developing fluency also emphasizes comprehension.

After Mastering Basic Partner Reading

Students and teachers like variety. Students progress at different levels and have different needs. This is where differentiation of the strategy comes into play.

Deeper Summarization: Always in pairs, and still switching back and forth reading aloud or silently reading, Partner A reads a sentence, Partner B then summarizes or restates the important point of the sentence. Partner B then continues with the next sentence, Partner A summarizes and continues with the following sentence. At the end of the paragraph, they summarize. We have even seen this as a fluency strategy where each partner commented on how well they read the sentence, how they self-corrected or used tone and intonation. Another variation is to have students do a Think-Aloud about what they are reading.

Paragraph by Paragraph: Partner A reads a paragraph. Partner B silently reads along helping as needed, then summarizes the paragraph always using Tier 2 and 3 words. Partner B then reads the next paragraph with help from Partner A. Partner A summarizes the paragraph. At the end of the page or subheading, both partners summarize the entire section, revisiting the text as needed to prove their version of the summarization.

One teacher had students do this version slightly different. Partners read a page alternating paragraphs. At the end of the page, Partner A retells what happened or summarizes facts from the first paragraph. Partner B then retells what happened or summarizes facts in the second paragraph, and so forth until they finish the page.

For Higher-Level Readers or Longer Texts: Partners remain next to each other, but after a paragraph or two of basic Partner Reading, partners silently continue with the text until they reach the bottom of the page, or the next subheading. Partners then put their heads together to orally summarize what they have read, returning, or rereading the text as needed.

If students are reading different texts, they still are paired and when they reach the end of the page or section, they still summarize what they read to their partner. This allows readers support when needed, but also shows that accountability is still required.

Choral Reading? Ok, But Only in Moderation

Students like to get creative with how they read. Choral Reading is not just for poetry or theater anymore! One U.S. Government class we observed after reading the text using standard Partner Reading, so that everyone at first had read through the text, decided they would read in unison by teams, one paragraph at a time. After a couple of times, they decided to start practicing their parts before class so they could outperform, out-read, the other teams. By practicing prosody in this fashion, the government content came to life. Some of the students who also had a physical science class together talked the teacher into letting them do the same in the science class. The science teacher took it a bit further and had whole-class rehearsals for reading and pronouncing words such as *elongated, ellipse,* and *perpendicular* so the choral reading would come out smoother. Both teachers reported that choral reading helped all students develop more confidence in using appropriate terminology and reassured ELs that help was necessary and available even for mainstream students. Choral reading also led students to explore new ways of presenting their unit products more creatively. Some decided to personify the solar system and presented with dialogue and movement what they had studied. The government teams also wrote short plays depicting a controversial event that blended history with politics.

Reciprocal Teaching and Reading

Reciprocal Teaching is an instructional strategy that takes the form of a dialogue between teachers and students regarding segments of text with the purpose of constructing the meaning of text. Reciprocal teaching is a reading technique developed to promote students' reading comprehension (Palincsar, 1986). This works well with more advanced English learners after they have practiced Partner Reading for a few weeks. Reciprocal approach calls for four specific reading strategies that are used to support comprehension: Questioning, Clarifying, Summarizing, and Predicting. Palincsar states that the purpose of reciprocal teaching is to facilitate a group effort between teacher and students, as well as among students in the task of bringing meaning to the text.

A word of caution here: Reciprocal Teaching follows a very scaffolded curve, beginning with high levels of teacher instruction, modeling, and input, which is gradually withdrawn to the point that students can use the strategies independently. Reciprocal teaching begins with the students and teacher reading a short piece of text together. In the beginning stages, the teacher models the "Fab Four" strategies required by Reciprocal Teaching, and teacher and students share in conversation to come to an agreement about the text (Williams, 2010).

The teacher then specifically and explicitly models his or her thinking processes aloud, using each of the four reading strategies. Students follow the teacher's model with their own strategies, also verbalizing their thought processes for the other students to hear. These are the typical roles in teams of four:

Summarizer—Highlights key ideas up to the point of where they have read

Questioner—Poses questions about unclear parts, puzzling information, connections to other concepts, and the big picture

Clarifier—Addresses confusing parts and attempts to answer questions posed by the team

Connector—Suggests how certain themes and concepts connect to other texts, theories, processes, or math solutions

Extra verbal discourse protocols need to be brought into every lesson for ELs. Otherwise, ELs may back away and contribute very little, regardless of the role they are assigned.

Literature Circles is very similar to Reciprocal Teaching since the aim is to encourage thoughtful discussions. Additionally, it requires that students comprehend what they are going to discuss and have sufficient mastery of words and sentence structures. Therefore, our recommendation is to begin with Partner Reading and Summarizing until ELs and peers are comfortable and confident enough to work in teams and are at English proficiency Level 4 or 5 before attempting Literature Circles. By then, ELs have developed sufficient discourse functions to handle literature discussions and contribute. We have seen many ELs sit back and not participate since it was too far above their proficiency level.

Summary

✓ The purpose of reading is to comprehend what has been read. Comprehension is vital regardless if the reason for reading is pleasure or to show understanding of a subject.

✓ Reading in the classroom for any learner should be a 100% high participation activity. It is a skill that must be explicitly taught, practiced, refined, revised, and finetuned.

✓ Reading with partners or in small groups fosters comprehension and motivation.

✓ It is not a silent, solitary activity to fill time. Reading well requires time, close analysis of the vocabulary and structure of the text being digested. It is a communal activity in the classroom regardless of the curriculum.

✓ ELs who are learning English as well as the curricula of their classes have a twofold purpose for reading. The support and structure of Partner Reading and Summarizing work well to help ELs process through the styles and academic language of each type and style of reading in every subject.

✓ All readers learn more, benefit more from cooperative learning, discourse, classroom discussions, practice, and rereading.

In the following chapter, we will discuss strategies designed for reentering the text, mining the text for evidence and opinion, and working as a group to comprehend the text, all with the intent of being able to answer text-based questions as proof of understanding.

Later in Chapter 7, vocabulary and reading culminate in writing to a source using text-based evidence with porosity.

6

After Initial Reading

The idea of teaching disciplinary literacy is quite different from the long-promoted content area literacy teaching. The latter has often championed the disciplinary literacy notion, but the result has been an emphasis on general comprehension skills and study skills, rather than apprenticing young readers into reading like disciplinary experts. K-W-L, three-level guides, Frayer model, 4-squares, etc., are all great teaching tools—they can enhance kids learning from text, but you are unlikely to find chemists or historians who use those approaches in their work. Thus, content area reading aims to build better students, while disciplinary literacy tries to get them to grasp the ways literacy is used to create, disseminate, and analyze information in the various disciplines.

—Shanahan (2017)

Consolidating Knowledge, Language, and Literacy

While Tim Shanahan may be referring to young readers in the opening quote to this chapter, he is describing what typically happens in secondary ESL/ELD classrooms. Teachers tell us that strategies such as the Frayer model, 4-squares, and KWL are fun, but take up too much precious time and do not help ELs comprehend reading in math, science, social studies, and ELA texts (online and in class) that core content teachers require.

"Students need ample opportunities for extended discussion of text meaning and interpretation" (National Academies of Science, Engineering, and Medicine [NAS], 2017 p. 282). We call those ample opportunities that are a perfect follow up to Partner/Triad Reading Crosscutting strategies for consolidating knowledge. By crosscutting we mean that they cut across all subjects and all parts of a lesson. For example, after Partner Reading, other student-centered and/or teacher-guided activities can be used to consolidate knowledge. Oral, written, or extension reading activities to anchor knowledge can be conducted through Cooperative Learning, journals, logs, and instructional conversations. These help to build redundancy of concepts and vocabulary—and those pieces of knowledge that will be tested. The strategies in this chapter are some of the favorite ones that can be used after Partner Reading with Summarization to integrate, create, consolidate, and dissect information, and most importantly thoroughly discuss it.

Debriefing as a Crosscutting Strategy

After about 15 minutes of Partner Reading or after working with any of the strategies we present in this book, the teacher asks students to pause where they are to debrief and begin a discussion of what they "have found so far." This open-ended question signals that students can *discuss themes, important details, and confusing pieces of text, question the author or the facts, and clarify concepts and key vocabulary.* The teacher usually ends the discussion with another open question, such as "What did you learn?" Besides content, students express lessons learned about *working together or things that did not work.*

Here is also where *deeper word study* can be infused. Perhaps there are extra words that you wanted to point out but that were not part of the preteaching at the top of the lesson. Did several students note a word or two they didn't understand? Or even reminders of grammar or words that you highlighted in Step 5 of the 7-Steps. Did you highlight a word for preteaching that has a different spelling when used as a plural or in a different tense? Is that word used in a different part of speech in a different piece of the text? How about those words that are easily taught with a gesture or realia? Making sure students are also paying attention to important Tier 3 words that may have in paragraph definition, for example "Entomologists—scientists that study bees …" works at this time too. Reminding students of the illustrations, charts, and or figures that are referred to in the piece they just read helps make connections to the reading and the vocabulary they are working to learn.

Teachers don't always debrief with the whole class. Sometimes they go from team to team and ask and probe. They conduct *instructional conversations* where students are welcomed to discuss, question, and think aloud about what they are working on. One middle school history teacher likes to pull five chairs together in a corner of the room and calls each team of four to come and converse with him for 10 minutes each. These rich conversations are always exciting. Students come prepared because although these are informal conversations, they like to show off their knowledge and even try to trip up the teacher with complex questions. The teacher uses this strategy before tests to get students to talk through the key ideas, details, and inferences from the social studies unit they have been reading and learning. These talk-through conversations help students go beyond answering literal questions about history to processing information at high levels of thought and meeting curriculum standards.

Cooperative Learning as a Crosscutting Strategy

The new NAS report on Promoting Success of Children and Youth (2017) proposes we "provide regular peer-assisted learning opportunities" (p. 283). *Cooperative Learning* has always been the undergirding strategy for all the Johns Hopkins University research on reading (Calderón, Hertz-Lazarowitz, & Slavin, 1998; Slavin, 1980; Slavin & Madden, 2001;). Cooperative Learning was the foundation for the 5-year Bilingual Cooperative Reading and Composition (BCIRC) matched experimental-control study. Instruction for the students in the five schools was conducted in English and Spanish using the same reading textbooks. After 2 years of implementation in second through fourth grades, 80% of the students in the BCIRC program met district exit/reclassification criteria. The final 20% met the criteria a year later. *Thus, it took only 2 to 3 years to learn English and exit into an all-English program.* Students continued at grade level through the fifth grade (Calderón et al., 1998, and What Works Clearinghouse). Since BCIRC consisted of teaching language, reading comprehension, and composition through Cooperative Learning methods, it became the basis for developing the six to twelfth grades Expediting Comprehension for English Language Learners (ExC-ELL).

Cooperative Learning is also the foundation of the 12 ExC-ELL components. It plays a major role before, during, and after reading components. After reading and discussing ideas with the teacher, the students work in teams of four to consolidate their knowledge and thinking. They can display their new words and knowledge into a group product or a final writing assignment. Graphic organizers lend themselves to this type of consolidation. Information learned can also be consolidated into written synopses or summaries. All products enable students to use the new vocabulary words again, anchoring meaning through utility. They use the words to map out concepts or to write the summaries. When a team finishes before the others, they drill each other on the meaning, spelling, and multiple meanings of the words.

Teachers usually prepare the students to work in teams from the beginning of the year until students learn to work efficiently. This involves gathering the ESL/ELD level of each of your students, checking to see where they are in the different domains of Speaking, Reading, Writing, and Listening. One composite score is not sufficient, as many times ELs need additional support or explicit instruction in reading or writing, while the other domains are near-native levels. Knowing each student's specific level in each domain will help to form those heterogeneous groups that help all learners succeed and ELs improve in the specified domains.

After reviewing each student's needs, teachers make sure each student has an academic task and learns. Assigning "one leader" does not work. The leader tends to do all the organizing, thinking, and even the work! Instead, start by assigning simple task activities so the focus is on learning how to work together and expect the best from all team members. Even the newcomer can contribute. Students always find tasks to bring ELs into the fold, in case you can't think of something. Post, present, discuss, review, and clarify as needed with students the following norms for working in teams:

- Everyone must contribute ideas.
- Everyone must work on all tasks.
- Everyone must show respect for peers.
- Everyone must learn and master the material.

Some teachers like to assign roles for more complex tasks or for analyzing text at a deeper level. Some examples that have explicit roles so that each student is responsible for an academic aspect of the task are the following:

- Content Connector—discusses connections between new and old information; between instructional objective and information being gathered

- Architect—responsible for graphing or combining meaningful pieces of information
- Vocabulary Collector—looks for key words and other interesting, unfamiliar, and perhaps relevant words on text or table tent and shares with the team
- Seeker—finds interesting, important, or puzzling pieces of information in the text to read aloud to the group for further discussion

After students have completed their team product and learned the new vocabulary and concepts, they write in their journals or Exit Passes how this information affects them or their environment or the world. Exit Passes or Exit Tickets are 2" x 3" cards where students write their reflection or a quick summary based on a teacher-provided prompt and hand it to the teacher as they leave the classroom. They can make connections to their lives and current events. They can also make connections to other chapters, literature, or discussions they have had in class.

Cooperative Summarizing Strategy

Class summaries help students review and remember information. Students can explain what they have learned through an oral summary that focuses on the main concept and key attributes of that concept. They can also write that summary at the end of the class period and submit it on an index card–size paragraph as an Exit Pass. One favorite way of summarizing in 5 minutes or less is to assign a number to each student in a team of four after they have read a sizable chunk of text. This is called an Oral Summary Round Table. Large pieces of text are parsed into two or three manageable chunks. After the signal, students begin their summaries.

Oral Summary Round Table

Student #1—Initially, the text section ...

Student #2—Following that, ...

Student #3—Subsequently, ...

Student #4—Finally, ...

Activity/strategy norms have been set in place such as "only one complete sentence per turn," "everyone participates—if someone says what you were going to say, repeat what you agree with," and "civil discourse is always used." The strategy continues until all sections are summarized. They can use their table tents that have additional transition words such as *afterward, in due course, thereafter, moreover,* and *notwithstanding,* or those civil discourse sentence starters of *I agree, I disagree,* etc.

Formulating Questions as a Crosscutting Strategy

When adolescents work in teams of four, it is important to give them challenging activities that keep them busy learning minute by minute. Figure 6.1 contains a Table Tent for Bloom's Taxonomy Level 4. (See our website www.ExC-ELL.com for several variations of this tool.) Each slide has key verbs, question stems, and activities for that particular level. For example, the verbs for the *Knowledge* category, which is basically for recalling or remembering information, are words such as *describe, define, identify, label, recognize.* However, for a higher category such as *Analyzing,* the verbs to be used are words such as *differentiate, distinguish,* or *select.* Questions for this category would be: What conclusions can you draw from … ? What

Figure 6.1   Bloom's Level 4

Thinking Process	Verbs for Objectives	Model Questions	Instructional Strategies
(Analyze) Breaking down into parts, forms	analyze categorize classify compare differentiate distinguish identify infer point out select subdivide survey	What is the function of … ? What's fact? Opinion? What assumptions … ? What statement is relevant? What motive is there? Related to, extraneous to, not applicable What conclusions? What does the author believe? What does the author assume? Make a distinction. State the point of view of …	• Models of thinking • Challenging assumptions • Retrospective analysis • Reflection through journaling • Debates • Discussions and other collaborating learning activities • Decision-making situations

is the function of … ? For Bloom's *Create* level, the type of products or activities for this would be: Design a … ; Make a flow chart for … (https://cft.vanderbilt.edu/guides-sub-pages/blooms-taxonomy/).

These table supports are given to the students to use throughout the semester. Instead of always answering book or teacher questions, students write the questions in teams. Formulating questions uses a much higher-order and complex thinking skill than just answering questions. Moreover, they really need to comprehend what they have read to be able to write the questions. Question stems are useful for constructing questions after Partner Reading to help students return to the text and delve deeper into comprehension. To test those questions, the students engage in a teacher-facilitated classroom debrief and discussion known as *Numbered Heads Together*. With Numbered Heads Together, students listen to their own questions, respond, elaborate, and have great academic arguments based on the text they are reading.

Combining Cooperative Learning With Close Reading

In a Numbered Heads Together strategy, each team of four writes two questions on the text they have been reading. Initially, they write one question from Bloom's knowledge, comprehension, or application category and another from the analysis, synthesis, evaluation, or create category. In addition to the questions, the teams must provide text-based answers for their questions. They write these questions and possible answers on an index card and then give them to the teacher. The teacher reviews the cards to make sure both questions and answers were provided and to see if modifications to the questions or answers are needed. The teacher then moderates a class discussion using the student generated questions for a Numbered Heads Together to test the class.

After creating the questions, the students number off from 1 to 4 in each team; the teacher calls out a question and asks all the teams to put their heads together to discuss the answer and make sure everyone knows the answer. After 2 minutes, the teacher calls a number, and a student from each team has to stand and respond for the whole team. Students continue to add to the answer until all teams have answered. This strategy is particularly helpful for ELs and newcomers because they know they must be ready to answer. The onus is on them and their teammates to be prepared to participate and since the expectation is that every team answers, students soon realize that they must prepare more than one answer and listen to their classmates' answers. The accountability factor works for the other students because they learn how to help the EL as well as prepare themselves more accurately. In a very short period of time, and with just four questions, every student has orally provided an answer, and 100% of the students have reviewed the text or material needed for the answer.

Later in the lesson, remaining questions are sometimes used with the *Conga Line* activity. The line can sometimes become two concentric circles, also known as Inside Outside Circles. In a Conga Line, students stand and face each other. In circles, students stand in two concentric circles and face each other. The teacher calls out a question and gives students a minute to review, discuss, and memorize each answer. Then she arbitrarily calls on one student to respond. The students then move to the next partner, and another question is discussed. Usually six to eight questions are used for this activity.

With each of these activities, students are also provided with and expected to use Accountable Talk or respectful discourse sentence starters. When responding to a classmate, students use transitions such as the basic *furthermore, in addition,* or *also,* but have ready examples of transitions that promote addition or refutation such as "I agree… ," "I disagree… ," "according to the text/author, …" And for those who need to repeat something that was already said, "I want to reiterate …" or " I want to echo …".

Better Than Other Assessments

When students formulate questions for such competitions, the questions tend to be at higher levels than textbook questions and are more motivating for the students. Usually, activities such as these become better assessments of student knowledge than the traditional paper and pencil tests. These activities also save teachers time trying to figure out what questions to ask and how to assess students.

There are many other Cooperative Learning activities that are applicable at any stage of the lesson delivery. Most chapters in this book integrate Cooperative Learning at different intervals and for different purposes.

After Reading Graphic Organizers as Crosscutting Strategies

Graphic organizers—also called cognitive organizers, semantic maps, webs, organizers, diagrams, graphs, charts, etc.—are visual representations of knowledge to help students comprehend content (Bromley, Irwin-DeVitis, & Modlo, 1995). Graphic organizers involve both visual and verbal information; they promote active learning and exercise students' use of language as they listen, think, talk, read, and write. They can also be tools for group interaction between teachers and students and among students. When explicitly taught, modeled, and discussed, graphic organizers integrate language and thinking to highlight key vocabulary in a visual display of knowledge that facilitates deeper discussion and sharing of ideas and information.

ExC-ELL teachers use graphic organizers to explain concepts for Tier 1, 2, and 3 words. Graphic organizers help ELs understand grade-level text without changing the meaning or lowering the academic and cognitive level of the content. For ELs, graphic organizers are best used as a review and consolidation strategy, when the learner has been provided all of the needed information. Used in teams or with a partner and with the expectation of course that everyone contributes, graphic organizers help modify difficult texts so that content is illustrated in a meaningful way for all students. The four basic patterns are

1. *Hierarchical.* The linear organizer includes a main concept and the levels of subconcepts under it.

2. *Conceptual.* The organizer consists of a central idea with supporting characteristics and/or examples. A Venn diagram is an example of conceptual organizer with two overlapping circles for representing information being compared.

3. *Sequential.* The organizer arranges events in chronological order with a specific beginning and end into chronology, or cause and effect, problem and solution, and process and product.

4. *Cyclical.* The organizer represents a series of events in a circular formation with no beginning or end, just a continuous sequence or successive series of events.

There are many books and Web sites for graphic organizers. By simply typing in "graphic organizers," the Web gave us many pages of sites (e.g., www.graphic.org; www.smartdraw.com; www.graphic.org; http://www.techlearning.com/blogentry/9736).

Final Debriefing and Formative Student Assessment

Most states now have a required formative assessment for ELs to be administered once a year to track their learning progress. Nevertheless,

The Council of Chief State School Officers (http://www.ccsso.org/Documents/2016/CCSSOELLUseGuidance20160829.pdf, 2016) recommends that other formative data be collected to have a more valid profile of each EL. We provide here the type of evidence that should come from the core content areas.

Performance Data Collection

You can document an EL's learning progress on language development, reading comprehension, and content learning. Keeping a portfolio of where your students started and where they are now helps show you, administrators, and most importantly, the students how far they have come. These data also help you plan lessons and show rationale for your supports and strategies and provide evidence of differentiation. You can randomly select a student once a week by using some of the criteria below.

Evidence of Language, Literacy, and Content Learning of ELs

- ✓ Observing/listening to partners during Step 6 of vocabulary instruction (appropriate use of the word, its pronunciation, providing four or more examples).
- ✓ Observing/listening to Partner Reading and recording fluency (intonation, pronunciation, prosody), miscues (consonant blends, word usage, idioms, verb tense), and engagement (focused on reading, time on task).
- ✓ Observing/listening to partner summaries after each paragraph to record (use of Tier 2 and 3 words, instances of contribution to summaries, and the quality of the summaries).
- ✓ Collect student-formulated questions (well-constructed, meaningful, creative).
- ✓ Collect written summaries and Exit Passes (points for use of new Tier 2 and 3 words, content concepts, cohesiveness).
- ✓ Make notations during Numbered Heads Together or other Cooperative Learning activities (social and collaborative skills such as participating, helping, accepting help, self-control, self-awareness).

Instructional conversations also serve to assess student oracy and comprehension. With the final debriefing through these conversations, the focus turns to the whole chapter, reading segment, or literature piece. Judgments are made about the author's purpose, point of view, quality, and clarity of the message, how important this information is, and how it connects to what is happening in the world today.

Debriefing aloud at the end of the period helps to consolidate language and content. Debriefing requires returning to the standards and expectations introduced at the beginning of the lesson. Students can be guided through the standards and expectations with simple questions such as "Remember our objective? What did we do today to help us meet this goal?" and followed by several usages of "What else?" to encourage the students to review and reiterate the learning. This strategy also helps the teacher to check lesson pacing and where to start the next lesson. Is there something that needs to be revisited? Did we get to all the content and activities we needed to? However, teachers often forget to debrief. They don't leave sufficient time before the bell rings. One teacher's solution was to set her timer to ring 10 minutes before the bell. This way she trained herself and her students to spend that time consolidating knowledge for that period and to gauge what needed to be revisited the next day. After a while, they didn't need the timer. It became inherent, and students automatically stopped to wait for the final instructional conversations with their teacher.

School Structures for Reading Success

As content teachers encounter more and more ELs and low-level readers in their classroom, it will not make sense to expect students to read on their own and comprehend. Moreover, it does not make sense to expect content teachers to become expert reading teachers on their own as they juggle teaching academic language, reading comprehension, and domain knowledge. Therefore, it is imperative that school administrations provide teachers and co-teachers with time to study how to integrate all this into their lesson plans. Core content teachers and ESL/ELD/bilingual teachers can work together to study their own lesson preparation and delivery. Teachers will need year-long ongoing support for learning the ideas set forth in this chapter and infusing them into their lessons. Teachers who were the most creative and most successful during the years of our BCIRC study were given time to get together in their learning communities. They were observed and coached by experts who had conducted or participated in a 10-day training. Their administrators were also trained to observe and support them. We have now adopted this model for

ExC-ELL schools. Successful students require successful teachers. Teachers who are supported continuously become continuous learners and transmit this to their students.

Summary

✓ Without reading instruction and follow-up activities from content area teachers, students get used to surface comprehension resulting in failing to thrive in the content.

✓ Interaction is critical for reading comprehension. When students read on their own and answer questions silently or only in writing, one can never really tell if they are understanding, learning content, or thinking at higher levels beyond literal responses. Having students create and answer questions based upon the text requires close reading and a deeper dive into the content.

✓ With explicit reading instruction from content area teachers, students develop critical comprehension, learn vocabulary continually, associate readings with prior knowledge, add new knowledge, interpret facts more accurately, and apply critical thinking to texts.

✓ Student progress on oracy and literacy can be assessed through observations and documentation.

7

Writing Increases and Consolidates Vocabulary, Reading, and Content Learning

Reading and writing are now essential skills in most white- and blue-collar jobs. Ensuring that adolescents become skilled readers and writers is not merely an option for America, it is an absolute necessity.

—Graham and Hebert (2010, p. 3)

Graham and Hebert (2010) go on to list many causes for their concerns about the lack of writing proficiency for most students. Here are only three of their main concerns:

- Forty percent of high school graduates lack the literacy skills employers seek.
- Lack of basic skills cost universities and businesses as much as $16 billion annually.
- Only 1 out of 4 twelfth-grade students is a proficient writer.

Secondary teachers are concerned about the lack of reading and writing skills of ELs as well as the native English striving readers and writers. They also tell us that their teacher preparation or preservice programs did not provide writing in the content courses. Secondary educators have rarely been taught the genres of writing. Now, they find they must teach to state standards that call for informational, argumentative, descriptive, sequential, or narrative writing that fits the standard being taught. Science, social studies, and math teachers are wanting to know how to explicitly teach to each of these types of writing to all their students.

Whether entering high school or preparing for college or a career, the ability to write clear, coherent, descriptive, and/or well-argued prose is imperative. Writing well is a keystone factor in demonstrating literacy in any language. The quality of writing influences all readers: teachers, classmates, prospective employers, clients, and colleagues alike, whether it is filling out an application form, writing a job related or scientific report, or even a simple lesson summary or Exit Ticket.

Students are now required to demonstrate their understanding of claims and evidence, often as presented in complex texts, as well as cogent and well-organized reactions to the topics or issues at hand. They are also required to show this evidence by correctly summarizing, applying, citing, and quoting these texts. This could be agreement, disagreement, or a general balanced critique of the texts, but regardless of the focus, the expectation for students in every subject is to show increasing mastery of writing that is structured around argument or explanation supported by specific evidence.

Most teachers are aware that ELs often have an incomplete knowledge base or a fragmented base of the formal writing processes. They haven't been explicitly taught to write and have missed reading comprehension skills that would help them analyze complex texts. ELs agonize for hours before writing because they don't even know how to start their sentences or paragraphs. In this chapter, we provide ideas, skill-building strategies, and tools for the whole writing process.

Louisa Moats (2017) states that the main issue with which ELs have trouble writing is that they learned how to fill in worksheets without really knowing what the words mean. So, meaning is the main issue. Therefore, she strongly advises combining oral language modeling, oral expression (discourse), talking about the words, and having the instruction be very interactive. In other words, a lot of dialogue and a lot of vocabulary instruction must be embedded in writing.

Evidence-Based Research on Writing Programs

The National Commission on Writing (2016) indicates that efforts to improve writing are virtually nonexistent in current attempts to reform schools. Writing skills need to be improved if students are to succeed in school, college, and life. In short, writing about a text enhances comprehension because it provides students with a tool for visibly and permanently recording, connecting, analyzing, personalizing, and manipulating key ideas in text.

There is lack of evidence for specific writing programs for elementary or secondary grades. Amazingly, most popular writing programs or writing workshops have not been tested with ELs. Some have even had negative effects on ELs (Gillespie & Graham, 2011). After extensive studies of writing commissioned by the Carnegie Corporation of New York, Graham and Hebert (2010) found that employing a specific combination of evidence-based instructional features is better than buying any program. The researchers made these recommendations for explicit instruction in writing for all students:

I. Have students write about the texts they read.

Students' comprehension of science, social studies, and language arts texts is improved when they write about what they read, specifically when they

- respond to a text in writing (personal reactions, analyzing and interpreting the text),
- write summaries of a text,
- write notes about a text, and
- answer questions about a text in writing, or create and answer written questions about a text.

II. Teach students the writing skills and processes that go into creating text.

Students' reading skills and comprehension are improved by learning the skills and processes that go into creating text, specifically when teachers teach

- the process of writing,
- text structures for writing, and
- paragraph or sentence construction skills.

III. Increase how much students write.

Students need to write in all subjects. Moreover, students' reading comprehension is improved by having them increase how often they produce their own texts.

Application and Modifications for ELs

In this chapter, we address how we took these features and tested them with ELs. We share here how they relate to "teaching writing to ELs" and their peers in secondary content classrooms. We found through our studies of ExC-ELL that in addition to the features identified by the Carnegie Corporation and the National Commission on Writing, effective instruction for ELs should also include:

➢ Vocabulary instruction before, during, and after reading from the text students are reading
➢ Oral language modeling by the teacher of sentence structures, and sentence connectors/transitions to be used
➢ Vocabulary and syntax taught at the beginning of a class period, which should be applied in exit passes at the end of the period
➢ Explicit step-by-step description of the sequence: drafting, revising, editing, writing a conclusion, and writing a powerful thesis statement and title
➢ Ample peer discussion about the words, text structures, text features, and purpose for writing
➢ Explicit modeling and instruction on note taking: how to write notes or annotate text
➢ Explicit modeling and instruction on how to write different types of summaries

You are probably beginning to see the relationship between the chapter on vocabulary and discourse, the chapters on reading, and this chapter on writing. We recommend that you share with your students many of the tools and Table Tents suggested in the vocabulary chapter as they begin their writing. Plus, we cannot emphasize enough the major role that close reading a subject-related text plays in the development of writing. With the vocabulary, reading, writing cycle, students also develop higher-order thinking and collaborative skills.

Writing Process in the Content Areas

Writing about science, math, and other types of information promotes students' learning of the material. In addition, teaching writing not only improves how well students write, but it also enhances students' ability to read a text accurately, fluently, and with comprehension (Graham & Hebert, 2010). For ELs, it also helps them develop academic vocabulary. Preteaching vocabulary at the beginning of each class period helps students comprehend what they read, read closely to learn the material, and then be ready to return to the text to begin writing. As they go back into the text to write, ELs learn more vocabulary and the features of writing the author employs (Calderón, Slakk, Carreón, & Peyton, 2017).

The process that has been most effective with ELs begins with teams of four. As noted before, collaborative/cooperative learning expedites language and literacy. After the ELs have mastered the routines of drafting, revising, and editing in quartettes, they work in triads, then pairs, then individually. If products during the writing in pairs is not up to standard, that is an indication that they need more exposure and practice in teams of four. The "four heads are better than one" approach yields more discussions (Sparks, 2017) and better learning of content and collaborative skills (Dewitt, 2017; Slavin, Madden, Calderón, Chamberlain, & Hennessy, 2009).

The Writing Process for ELs and Striving Writers

We are sharing the phases of the writing process the way we present them to the teachers in our training session, and the way teachers should present them to the students. The workflow as presented below not only helps students follow along, but it also helps the teachers conduct the process fluidly. As with all instructional processes, especially with newly introduced concepts, expectations, or strategies, explicit instructions and clarifying and modeling of the skills and steps are crucial. The following strategies need to be explicitly introduced, practiced, refined, and debriefed with the students, showing them the connections to both the content and why the students are using the strategy.

Drafting and Brainstorming

Write-Around

In this strategy, students work in teams to jointly create a piece of writing as a response to a prompt. They are ready to do this since they have been expecting to write about what they have been reading, using the key vocabulary they have been taught and practiced with the 7 Steps, read and used in their partner reading and summaries. They have discussed facts, the author's evidence, purpose, and opinion when they returned to the text for their student created text-based questions, and then answered the same via a whole-class discussion or a Numbered Heads Together class debrief. Here are the steps and a few notes on the strategy:

- Students form teams of three or four.
- Students clear their desks of all materials and obstructions. (The Table Tents with connectors, transition words, or other words students are required to use, stay on the table.)
- Each student has one paper and a pen or pencil.
- Each student writes the prompt provided by the teacher and completes a sentence based on the knowledge derived from the text(s) they have been reading. (*Example Prompt: Humans are the cause of global warming due to . . .* or if students have a choice, they need to choose which prompt they will work on as a team and put that at the top of their papers.)
- After completing the sentence, each student passes the paper to his or her peer on the right. The goal is to stay on the topic of study and use related Tier 2 and Tier 3 words. Invented spelling is OK at the time of drafting. We don't want anyone apprehensive or slowing down because of spelling. Students will get to fix spelling later.
- The student receiving the paper reads what is written, adds one sentence to connect with what has been written by others, and passes the paper to the right.
- The process continues until the teacher calls time (usually 10 to 12 minutes).

After 10 to 12 minutes of team writing, each team should have at least three-fourths of a page filled. If not, give them a few more minutes. They need to have sufficient writing to revise and edit. All students are responsible for writing a sentence during each round. Nobody passes. Not even the Newcomers. In some cases, the teacher twins a Newcomer with another student, and the Newcomer repeats what the other student has written—they need this practice. In other cases, the teacher lets the Newcomer keep the book open or lets them use a sheet with key concepts and words and the Table Tents. If allowing Newcomers to have a source to reference, limit the time for each round to encourage continual movement. One teacher who has only Newcomers gives 1 minute during each round to write each sentence for the first 2 weeks. Their expectation is to fill at least half a page. She times them because some take too long to get started. The 1-minute timing can gradually be removed as the Newcomer becomes more secure in his or her writing and have internalized the appropriate timing for getting his or her ideas on paper.

Be reassured that Newcomers can handle this. Remember that you already taught quite a few words and that the Newcomer read in a triad, participated in a Numbered Heads Together, or similar Cooperative Learning activities and learned quite a bit of words, phrases, and sentence structures that are relevant to the topic of the writing. High expectations and rigor are the norm for Newcomers. They have so little time to catch up. They are eager to catch up. Let's give them the tools to hit the road running! There is no such thing as "a silent period." ELs remain silent when they don't have the tools and an instructional process that facilitates their engagement. In Kingsbury Middle School, Shelby County schools in Memphis, we observed a Newcomer participate in this process her first day of school. The teacher paired her with another EL, and both were delighted to participate. The EL felt special because she was asked to help; the Newcomer felt confident because she had help and felt successful since she had used English and participated in the class that very day. That team's final product was as elaborate as the other teams' products and met all the criteria.

Strategy Process Notes: Beginning the Write-Around

Display, discuss, and summarize these steps in your PowerPoint slides with the students when you start teaching them this strategy and as a review from time to time when new students arrive:

Write-Around

- Form teams of three or four.
- Clear your desks of all materials and obstructions.
- Everyone needs one paper and a pen or pencil.
- Everyone writes the prompt and completes a sentence based on the knowledge from what you have been reading.
- After completing the sentence, pass the paper to your classmate on the right.
- When you receive the paper from your teammate, read what is written, add one sentence to connect with what has been written by your classmates, and pass the paper to the right.
- Stay on the topic and use the Tier 2 and Tier 3 words we have been working with. Don't worry about spelling right now.
- Keep going until I call time.

When students are first learning this strategy, there are a few extra procedural points to learn. Provide students with plenty of paper and extra writing implements. The extra paper is for when the team's creation fills a whole sheet of paper. When this happens, rejoice! They are writing a lot, but since they will later literally "cut-n-paste," we want them to use a fresh piece of paper rather than turn it over and keep going on the back. Be sure to have them pass around both pieces of paper as a set. Additionally, in the beginning, students may need a review of passing to the right. We have found that even for adults, we need to practice this first before beginning the writing.

We have also had students who say they have finished their narrative before time is up. One of our colleagues tells them to write the sequel. In other words, keep writing until the teacher says time is up. When starting with whole classes or larger populations of Newcomers in a classroom, two sentences each is enough to get started. Later make the expectation three, the next week four, and so on until you no longer have to have a minimum.

R.A.F.T.

R	A	F	T
News reporter	College-educated adults	News article	Global warming
Acute triangle	Obtuse triangle	Travel guide	Differences between triangles along the trip
Elon Musk	Government officials	Report	How electric cars are better
Rosa Parks	Self	Journal	Why I made the choices I did

R.A.F.T. is another writing/drafting technique that can be used with any subject as a brainstorming strategy. The purpose of R.A.F.T. (Role, Audience, Format, Topic) is to produce clear and coherent writing in which the development, organization, and style are appropriate to task, purpose, and audience.

R = role (Who are you as a writer?): Allows students to take on a variety of roles to explore different points of view.

A = audience (To whom are you writing?): The audience is clearly defined.

F = format (What form will the writing take?): Essay, speech, letter, dialogue, memo, etc.

T = topic (What is the subject?): Must be narrow enough so students are not overwhelmed.

Initially, ELs work in pairs with non-ELs, writing R.A.F.T.s and later in triads or teams of four to practice. They apply the skills of drafting, Ratiocination, and Cut-n-Grow. In fact, after having gone through the first Write-Around with all its phases, students should continue to apply editing and revising to all the writing assignments in every class. Once they have practiced a skill, mechanic, or structure of English, it becomes an expectation.

Strategy Process Notes: R.A.F.T.

Students can be involved in this strategy after they have been taught the basic components of Role, Audience, Format, and Topic. In teams, they create each of the four components and then write about them, or share with the class allowing all to choose from the combined list. See our website www.ExC-ELL.com for a R.A.F.T. Table Tent example.

Moving on to Revisions

Read-Around-Aloud for Write-Around or R.A.F.T. Part 2

After students have written a sufficient amount of text (either with Write-Around or R.A.F.T.), it is time to share all that hard work. Give students about 5 minutes to take turns reading the composition that ended up in front of them when you called time. Each composition belongs to the whole team, not to the one who wrote the first sentence. Here are the instructions (Remember to display these instructions, debrief and summarize them. Ask your students: Why are we doing this? How does this help you?):

- Students do a Read-Around-Aloud.
- Read the composition you are holding to your team. (Use your Level 1 voices.)
- Select the one your team likes the best. This is the one you will revise and edit as a team.

After reading all the papers, they select the one the team likes the best to share with the whole class. We call this the "star" paper and have everyone who worked on it write his or her name on it. This is the paper the whole team will revise and edit. Hold on to the other papers; some students like to take things from other papers and add them to the star paper. Additionally, some teachers ask students to do Ratiocination (later in this chapter) on each of the papers they are holding so they get more practice. In the end, they will all work on one composition.

Strategy Process Notes: Read-Around-Aloud—Setting the Tone

When explicitly teaching this strategy, it may take some students time to get used to working in teams and not "owning" a product. See the next section for the benefits of working in teams. At the start, it is always good to remind the students that everyone owns the compositions, no one is at fault, mistakes happen, this is just the beginning of the writing process, and that they will have time and opportunity to improve it.

On the other hand, it will also be important to convey that the expectation is that the writing will be added to and improved and that writing is not a one-and-done process. One easy way to do that is for you, the teacher, to model the process, maybe with some of your own writing. Susan Neuman (2017) suggests that teachers themselves practice writing and work with each other to self-teach about writing and even form a "writers' club" as part of the teacher learning community.

Ratiocination

This strategy explicitly teaches grammar and academic composition within the writing process. It is a systematic way for students to re-enter their papers and begin revising. Here are some examples; please teach only one at a time. The process like writing is circular. Every 6 weeks, six or more strategies can be taught and later revisited. By the end of the semester, all students will be self-directed and self-evaluative in their writing assignments across the subject areas.

- Teacher asks students to box the first word in every sentence. Then, they count how many initial words are repeated, such as *the, they, because,* and then change one or two maximum to a more sophisticated sentence starter (*additionally, therefore, subsequently*).
- Teacher asks the students to check their papers for overuse of some Tier 1 words in sentences, such as *good, and, nice, I,* and change to Tier 2 words or phrases. This is a good time to return to the Mentor Text and find words that the author uses.
- Teacher may need to do a mini-lesson before the students check for an element of grammar (*past tense, compound sentences,*

incomplete sentences, punctuation). Or remind students of the grammar or mechanics piece they highlighted in the lesson's Think-Aloud.

- Students can highlight all the repeated words.
- Students can underline in two different colors alternate sentences to make visible the length of the sentences.
- They can circle all the verbs and check for verb tense or subject–verb agreement.
- They can check for proper spelling of targeted vocabulary.

Strategy Process Notes: Ratiocination

Students should have highlighters, colored markers, pencils, or crayons available for this strategy. The teacher starts by having students check for only one feature per paper (per writing assignment) and adds more as the students learn the process and additional aspects of grammar. This process is also a group process and involves team discourse. As stated earlier, for extra practice, some teachers like to have all students practice Ratiocination with the paper each one is holding.

Teachers can also individualize Ratiocination by assigning targeted features that a Newcomer or a Long-Term EL needs to practice fixing. In our training, we display a rubric as part of the PowerPoint (a copy of which can be found on our website www. ExC-ELL.com). However, there are numerous items that can and should be ratiocinated. Some variations and tweaks on our standard example have been to circle the verb, box the noun, and draw a line from subject to verb and verify correct subject-verb agreement. For those students whose first language doesn't use the conventions of capitalization or punctuation marks, students can color the periods or other punctuation marks if they are there; if not, it will become visible immediately.

Cut-n-Grow

Some students are hesitant about doing rewrites and complete overhauls of their writing. Cut-n-Grow allows students to do a focused rewrite without completely rewriting everything. In this strategy, students literally cut their writing at a place they want to improve, rearrange, elaborate upon, or add evidence to support what is already written. After inserting the new details, they reattach the rest of the text.

Strategy Process Notes: Cut-n-Grow

Many teachers like to plan their lessons so that there is a break after Ratiocination and before Cut-n-Grow. This allows them to collect the drafts and review the progress of students to this point, but also to make copies of the original compositions before they are cut up. We've known teachers who do this right after Read-Aloud-Around. Since some schools use iPads and other technology, some teachers (and even students) take pictures of the composition throughout the cycle to show the steps of the process.

One caveat is that this strategy is meant to be done with one or two rewrites or add-ons maximum. Students (and our adult training participants too) like to cut and may cut every sentence—this distracts from the purpose of the strategy. It is important to emphasize that this is a *one-sentence/change-at-a-time activity*. Otherwise they will never be done.

In addition to their compositions, students will need scissors for each team, additional colors of copy paper or construction paper, and tape or glue stick. Now, here are the instructions:

- Using the star paper, find a sentence that needs to be followed with evidence, a claim or counterclaim. Some sentences might need elaboration or a quotation. All can be done with Cut-n-Grow.
- Cut compositions right after the sentence where you are going to add evidence from the text.
- The additional sentence(s) are written on the colored paper. Once written, tape the rest of the composition below the colored paper.
- Reread the improved body of the composition. If more Ratiocination or spell-check is needed, this is the time to do so.
- Once the body is written, revised, and given a final edit, write a powerful conclusion and a fantastic attention-grabbing title.

(See our website at www.ExC-ELL.com for a variety of examples and pictures of our strategies.)

Writing a Powerful Conclusion (Write-Around or R.A.F.T. Part 3)

Knowing when and how to end a piece of writing is as important as starting it. The introduction and the conclusion bookend the writing, the thoughts presented and should serve to bring home the author's opinion, reinforce the authority of the author's evidence, or inspire the reader to action. The conclusion is the final impression the reader has of that piece of writing. ELs need to have the art of conclusion writing explicitly taught, especially when different subjects call for slightly different criteria for the conclusion. Here are a few examples we have collected. Each content will have its own specific standards. The basic English language has cross-curricular standards for all types of writing, which we will discuss in Chapter 8.

A biology teacher provided this checklist:

Scientific Conclusion Paragraph Check List

- ☐ *Purpose* of experiment is explained.
- ☐ *Steps* of experiment are described.
- ☐ *Similarities and differences* in data are described.
- ☐ *Hypothesis* is restated and compared to results.
- ☐ *Explanation of results* used to explain the uneven temperatures of the Earth.

Language arts and social studies teachers like to use:

- ☐ Restate the main idea or reaffirm your position.
- ☐ Synthesize the main points to show how they support your position.
- ☐ Offer a solution, make a call to action, suggest results or consequences, or leave the reader with an interesting final image.

It is a good idea to have available for the teams Table Tents, charts, and posters that have checklists along with the appropriate sequence, transition, and concluding words or phrases. (See our website at www.ExC-ELL.com for an example of Table Tents.) By this point in the process, students may not need them, but it is good scaffolding for Newcomers who may have just arrived and are at a lower English language development level.

Giving It a Powerful Title (Write-Around or R.A.F.T. Part 3 Continued)

The title needs to entice the reader to choose this piece of text to read. Think of the titles you may see on a newsstand or a gossip website. The titles are catchy, brief, thought provoking, or even shocking. Many times, they make use of onomatopoeia or alliteration to catch the eye of the potential reader. For creative writing and practicing these writing strategies, this is great and is a good way to show the principles of a good title. Academic writing of specific genres will have its own individual standards that emphasize how the title is an important insight into the written work. We like to tell students to wait until they finish their compositions, since many times, the writing and conclusion set the tone for the title.

Strategy Process Notes: Conclusions, Titles, and Polishing

Two words: Table Tents! Make sure to provide sufficient support for all writers and all aspects of writing. Practicing some of the written discourse as we have discussed in previous chapters helps students prepare for creating the written word, but that in and of itself is not enough. In addition, you will need to work with your students to help them internalize these components because come test time, the Table Tents and posters and other supports are removed. Have practice sessions where they write what they can without the Table Tents and then use some of the revising and editing strategies to have them review their own writing and add those wonderful starters, transitions, and connectors.

Publishing, Celebrating, and Debriefing (Write-Around or R.A.F.T. Part 4)

After the conclusion and title, it is time to celebrate all of the students' hard work. Give your students the opportunity to share their masterpieces with the class. Give them a few minutes to practice reading what the team has written. Some will need help reading some of the handwriting perhaps or practice with pronunciation and fluency, but as a team, they will need to be ready to read aloud their creations. This is an important expectation, accountability piece, and a great way to celebrate their achievement.

When all have shared, post the revised, edited work in all of its glorious changes and growth. Some teachers will post this piece of work along with the cleaned up and beautified version of the text since a finalized piece of writing is the expectation of some standards. It is important for the students to see the steps of the writing process from the original draft to the result of all their hard work. This is what administrators and parents are looking for too.

To close the writing process, students and the teacher need to debrief the entire process from beginning to end. Review the writing process and all its steps. For each step, ask the students what they learned about the writing process and the content. Ask them to process through how each step helped them learn what they learned.

Social-Emotional Skill Development

Working in teams of four on each part of the writing process helps all students develop social and cooperative skills such as compromising, consensus, checking for understanding, withholding disappointment or anger when their sentences are being revised, as well as helping and accepting help. These skills cannot be developed when students are working individually. Peer interaction is the best way of developing interpersonal and behavioral skills. When students write with peers, their thinking is clarified, and more language is learned as they negotiate, reiterate, and clarify, or simply argue a fact or evidence. ELs learn to listen to peers, and non-EL peers learn to appreciate, relate to the experiences of ELs, respond to their emotions, and work with ELs. This is where students learn to value diversity.

As ELs and non-ELs work on the editing and revising phases, students learn how to give feedback and accept feedback. They continue to discuss and work together to improve their drafts. This in turn helps them develop self-management and responsible decision making. But, students do not automatically cooperate while in teams. There is a huge difference between "cooperative or collaborative learning" and "working in groups." *Cooperative/collaborative learning* means everyone is engaged and learning. *Working in groups* sometimes means sitting together but doing individual work, asking for help occasionally or copying. Here are some classroom norms that can be taught and posted on the wall or on a Table Tent:

1. Accept others' ideas for writing, revising, and editing.

2. Appreciate everyone's efforts.

3. Value experiences and contributions by Newcomers.

4. Keep trying and learning new words.

5. Learn to manage your emotions and feedback.

When students are required to practice these norms in the majority of their classrooms, by the end of the semester, they learn personal and social responsibility, to be flexible and self-evaluative. Some teachers assign grades or points for the skills they expect to see.

Summary

✓ Writing that is connected to the text or content is an easy assessment of understanding, but only if the writer has been *explicitly taught the process of good writing*.

✓ Writing is a learned skill that takes practice and re-visitation.

✓ Each step of the writing process needs explicit instruction, modeling, and practice and more practice.

✓ Teachers should be modeling their own writing for students to see.

✓ For ELs or any student, writing is not a solitary activity. Team writing takes the pressure off and helps develop congeniality.

✓ Writing comes after preteaching of vocabulary for comprehension of the text, modeling of structure and mechanics, and classroom discussion for deeper comprehension about the subject being written.

8

Diving Deeper
Into Writing

With any combination of teaching strategies, a teacher chooses to use, students must be given ample time to write. Writing cannot be a subject that is short-changed or glossed over due to time constraints. Moreover, for weaker writers, additional time, individualized support, and explicit teaching of transcription skills (i.e., handwriting, spelling, typing) may be necessary. For all students, teachers should promote the development of self-regulation skills. Having students set goals for their writing and learning, monitoring and evaluating their success in meeting these goals, and self-reinforcing their learning and writing efforts puts them in charge, increasing independence and efficacy.

—Gillespie and Graham (2011)

Writing and Critical Thinking

Writing intelligently about something is good proof of learning. Students can meet writing standards by doing their *reports, essays,* and *creative representations* in a style that is aligned to a writing standard or goal. It is easier to start ELs with descriptive writing in science, social studies, and language arts. Descriptive writing is easier for ELs because they have the Mentor Text they have been reading, plus the vocabulary bank they have been storing in their heads as the teacher takes them through the ExC-ELL lesson components #1 through #9. They have acquired sentence frames that the teacher pointed out in the Think-Aloud such as:

> This sentence has the word however at the beginning. So, I need to back up and read the sentence before. It says, "The weather channel said there was a 50% chance of rain. However, the humidity indicator is low." Students, at the end of our class, I want you to write a sentence using however in your Exit Ticket.

Using Prompts or Sentence Starters

The teacher has also given the students a *writing prompt* to get them started. *Stimulus-based prompts* need to align to the most current standards to develop students' critical analysis and writing skills. Prompts ought to involve complex performance tasks that require students to read, analyze, and reference related passages from what they have been reading to inform their writing. Stimulus-based prompts underscore the close relationship between reading and writing as students complete a first draft and revise to complete a final product.

For instance, when the students were reading about climate change, the prompt became: *"Changes in climate are mostly due to . . ."* The sentence starter or prompt is challenging enough and should generate a lot of thinking connected to what they have been reading. Students also like choices. Sometimes teams take sides with prompts that can lead to lively debates. Is climate change due to mother nature? Is it due to human causes? Aren't humans part of nature? Prove it. After writing is completed, teams can have debates and continue to research the topic.

Rubrics and Evidence of Learning

A final editing sweep and ways of evaluating reports or any writing assignment should be consistent across content domains. For example, formats for writing position papers can be given, along with information from the Web on opposing views on a government policy, an environmental issue, a way to solve a mathematical problem, or play/movie reviews. Rubrics can also be shared across disciplines such as the following example.

Final Editing and Revising Suggestions

- ☐ Your ideas are organized in a logical way.
- ☐ You clearly presented your argument.
- ☐ You illustrated your points with clear examples.
- ☐ All of your paragraphs relate to this topic.
- ☐ You have an introduction and a logical conclusion.
- ☐ Your sentences are clear and complete.
- ☐ You used transition words or phrases.
- ☐ You used Tier 2 and 3 words to express your ideas.
- ☐ You double checked your spelling, capitalization, grammar, and punctuation.

Developing Self- and Collective Efficacy

Other ways of evaluating a piece of writing is to have teams evaluate their own work or other team's work. This helps students develop a collective conscience about self-correction. In addition to using rubrics for the writing, students can grade themselves on their social norms (everyone contributed in all phases, we accepted and gave feedback respectfully, we learned that …).

Text Features, Text Structures, and Writing Products

Students love to skip over text features such as captions, cut outs, or timelines. These components of text are important to good writing technique. As they may have never been pointed out, it is therefore important to explicitly show how features enhance writing. During the teacher's Think-Aloud, features can be pointed out and with suggestions on how students can use one or two in their own writing. These are perfect additions for the Cut-n-Grow strategy. Chapter 4 presents a list of the text features and text structures.

While Chapter 4 illustrates text structures and their Tier 2 vocabulary, the most prevalent text structures that correlate with state standards are *argumentative, informative/explanatory,* and *narrative.* See Figure 8.1 for a list of some of the cognitive tasks to consider for each.

There are several prevalent text structures that cut across all subjects: *description, sequential, problem/solution, cause and effect, compare/ contrast,* and of course, *persuasive or argumentative* structures. Authors regularly use more than one or combine several structures. Teachers sometimes call them text types or genre. They also use different terms for the same final product.

Figure 8.1   Cognitive Tasks

Argumentative	Informative/Explanatory	Narrative
To what extent …	Analyze	Describe
Defend …	Explain	Identify
Pros and cons	Examine	Outline
Take a stand	Evaluate	Show

Figure 8.2   Variations of Writing Products

technical manual	history book style	math book style
science book style	chronology	scientific process
web sites	poetry	screenplay
short story	mystery novel	marketing plan
reflection journals	learning logs	summaries
narrative	note taking	exit ticket

The final products can also vary across content domains—some topics lend themselves to dramatizations; others to posters, fliers, newspaper articles; others to community reach-out such as booklets, pamphlets, or technical reports with Web-based information. See Figure 8.2 for some examples. In Kauai, the biology teacher took her class to the computer lab at the end of a unit for a week. Her students searched the Web for related information in teams, then, pulled it together to finalize a team product. Another middle school ended a multidisciplinary unit with an Amazing Race where teams competed with a mixture of content, word knowledge, and physical challenges. Everyone enjoyed those days, and all students felt accomplished.

Standards for Writing Across the Curriculum

Standards require that students incorporate narrative elements effectively into arguments and informative/explanatory texts. In history/social studies, students must be able to incorporate narrative accounts into their analyses of individuals or events of historical importance. In science and technical subjects, students must be able to write precise enough descriptions of the step-by-step procedures they use in their investigations or technical work that others can replicate and reach the same results.

Most state standards call for students to follow process and criteria as our examples below. These can be incorporated into your lesson plans and for students to follow as a checklist. These can also be used as criteria for grading the writing.

Some criteria can be combined or stand alone. Newcomers and other ELs can begin by focusing on one criterion only, accompanied by one item to ratiocinate and a simple Cut-n-Grow.

Samples for Selecting Writing Criteria/Rubric

- ✓ Write arguments focused on *discipline-specific content*. (The texts students have been reading.)
- ✓ Introduce claim(s) about a topic or issue, acknowledge and distinguish the claim(s) from alternate or opposing claims, and organize the reasons and evidence logically.
- ✓ Support claim(s) with logical reasoning and relevant, accurate data and evidence that demonstrate an understanding of the topic or text using credible sources.
- ✓ Use words, phrases, and clauses to create cohesion and clarify the relationships among claim(s), counterclaims, reasons, and evidence.
- ✓ Establish and maintain a formal style.
- ✓ Provide a concluding statement or section that follows from and supports the argument presented.
- ✓ Write informative/explanatory texts, including the narration of historical events, scientific procedures/experiments, or technical processes.
- ✓ Introduce a topic clearly, previewing what is to follow; organize ideas, concepts, and information into broader categories as appropriate to achieving purpose; include formatting (e.g., headings), graphics (e.g., charts, tables), and multimedia when useful to aiding comprehension.
- ✓ Develop the topic with relevant, well-chosen facts, definitions, concrete details, quotations, or other information and examples.
- ✓ Use appropriate and varied transitions to create cohesion and clarify the relationships among ideas and concepts.
- ✓ Use precise language and domain-specific vocabulary to inform about or explain the topic.
- ✓ Establish and maintain a formal style and objective tone.
- ✓ Provide a concluding statement or section that follows from and supports the information or explanation presented (http://www.corestandards.org/ELA-Literacy/W/7/).

Standards for Research to Build and Present Knowledge:

✓ Conduct short research projects to answer a question (including a self-generated question), drawing on several sources and generating additional related, focused questions that allow for multiple avenues of exploration.

✓ Use technology, including the Internet, to produce and publish writing and present the relationships between information and ideas clearly and efficiently.

✓ Gather relevant information from multiple print and digital sources, using search terms effectively; assess the credibility and accuracy of each source; and quote or paraphrase the data and conclusions of others while avoiding plagiarism and following a standard format for citation.

✓ Draw evidence from informational texts to support analysis, reflection, and research (http://www.corestandards.org/ELA-Literacy/W/7/).

Writing in the Content Areas

Writing in Social Studies Classrooms

Writing is evidence of thinking, therefore writing must be an important component of all social studies classes. Critical thinking and writing help students learn and provide evidence that learning has taken place.

Social studies teachers typically ask students to write five-paragraph narrative, persuasive, and analytical/argumentative essays. Students are usually asked to read and scrutinize an essay question, address all parts of the question, write a clear thesis in response to the question, and link historical information to the question. For such a writing task, teachers need to start by providing Mentor Text reading models and explicitly teach key Tier 2 task verbs like *compare/contrast, analyze, evaluate, justify,* and *assess the validity,* so that student writing matches what the prompt is asking them to do. ELs will also need model sentences that the teacher points out in the Mentor Text.

Writing in Science Classrooms

Learning science is much more complex than memorizing terms. Increasing student science literacy means that students need opportunity to process their ideas by discussing, debating, and writing—before, during, and after new learning takes place. This can be done through discussions or in writing (Duschl, 2007).

Writing like a scientist means being able to write clearly and effectively. Scientists have to keep clean and complete records of their ideas and work; so do lab students. However, writing in science is not just recording notes and/or listing data collected. Students must be expected to include reflections, questions, predictions, and claims linked to evidence and/or conclusions when they write (Duschl, 2007). For ELs, reading and analyzing these text conventions are absolutely necessary—they must have them explicitly pointed out and taught to them. Scientists communicate their findings to world-wide audiences or write grant applications and share their findings. Students learn all these types of writing by sharing their findings and interacting with peers throughout the writing process.

Writing in Mathematics Classes

Learning mathematics is also more than just memorizing sets of facts and doing basic operations. Writing in mathematics and engineering classes is the process to help students improve their thinking abilities to learn and communicate mathematics, engineering concepts, and creativity. Writing serves as a tool for learning to organize, analyze, and communicate mathematical ideas and to display acquired information. Appropriate content vocabulary should be used always—Tier 2 as well as Tier 3. Of course, the accuracy of the mathematical content is important; however, it is just as important to note errors in grammar, spelling, and punctuation through Ratiocination.

Writing in Language Arts

In language arts classes, ELs learn to clarify, define, and explain various points of view clearly and accurately on a topic with facts, definitions, comparisons, concrete details, and other information relating to the topic. ELs also learn to make a case for a specific course of action or point of view through valid reasoning and logical argument using relevant and sufficient facts to support the recommended action or position. They learn to read alternate forms of text such as illustrations, graphs, and other visuals. The student is therefore expected to write to tell a story or relate an incident or experience to entertain or to illustrate a point, real or imaginary, using story elements, structure, details, and language to support a rich and meaningful narrative.

ELs learn to combine all these features of reading while they are also learning English. Therefore, it is critical to slow down and let ELs and all students delve deeply into complex texts by the analysis and critical thinking involved in close reading. ELs can begin with simpler versions of a text, but should be expected to apply the same text features and structures.

All new assessments have questions that ask students to do some profound question analysis as described in this chapter. It comes down to analyzing various types of passages to identify the author's craft. The more students practice writing this way, the better they will do on the state exams! Here are some examples of a starter instruction and focusing questions for close reading.

Go back to the passage and analyze text features and structures to answer the following:

1. *What is the author saying?* (theme, ideas, main message, what did the main character learn?)

2. *How is the author saying it?* (language usage: figurative language, argumentative, polysemous words; motivation: jealousy, power, generosity; character attitude: humble, modest, superior; how is narrator different from his opponent: words, thoughts, body language?)

Of course, the test question won't have the tips in parentheses; thus, it is important that these elements be explicitly taught and students practice using them in their own writing. ELs can write routinely using a range of discipline-specific strategy-aligned tasks, purposes, and audiences in smaller pieces of writing. For example, they can write shorter pieces that ask them to

- Define
- Give an example
- Explain why
- Support your explanation with evidence
- Describe a solution
- Describe advantages and disadvantages
- Choose

Collective Efficacy

Teachers need to have an overall sense of the expected progression in writing over time for ELs. ESL/ELD teachers can help plan instruction for ELs at different levels of writing skill development. This will assist writing instruction to be consistent toward common goals, across subjects and teachers. For ELs, practice alone is insufficient—the practice must be aimed at some defined and consistent goal regardless of a student's developmental level or subject area. The ESL/ELD teacher can help during the writing process by teaching mini lessons on writing elements. Nevertheless, mini lessons need to be relevant to ELs' needs.

Most important, peer writing benefits all students. Writing-to-learn in teams fosters academic language, critical thinking, requiring analysis and application, and other higher-level thinking skills for ELs and all students. In the Write-Around phase, attention is focused on ideas rather than correctness of style, grammar, or spelling. This frees students to focus on thinking as they read what has been written by another student before they ponder carefully on what they will add. Continuing to work in teams to edit-revise-edit helps students focus on common mistakes and ways to correct them through peer input.

Writing that demonstrates knowledge cannot be a one-and-done activity. As we think back on our college papers, we can remember how many times we attempted to revise and edit. Likewise, our students need to experience the process whether in biology, history, or English class. Good writing needs to be preceded by good reading. Reading serves as a model of the genre they are supposed to use. Students need mentor texts in all subjects. Listening to lectures, watching video clips, or working on math operations without reading and deciphering problems does not generate thinking and academic writing. If writing is part of the benchmark assessments, then the writing students produce in class should mirror what is called for in the assessments. When all content teachers use the same techniques, formats, or templates around the same time, it makes it easier for all students to quickly grasp those formats.

Summary

✓ When students learn academic writing in teams, they feel more comfortable expressing themselves and worry less about making mistakes. Becoming aware of mistakes followed by self-correction is necessary to make progress.

✓ If we expect students to write in a subject content area, we must teach them the specifics of that style of writing and have them practice that style of writing.

✓ Setting the scene for students to succeed in writing also means teaching students the skills of collaboration where they develop social and emotional skills: self-management, self-awareness, responsible decision-making, social awareness, and relationship skills. At the individual student level, that means students practice listening to others, receiving feedback, giving feedback respectfully, etc.

✓ Another unexpected benefit from collaborative writing is that students develop positive relationships during the process. It also nurtures individual and group accountability.

✓ Most important, students learn how to develop academic writing skills.

9

Setting the Context for Success

If educators' realities are filtered through the belief that they can do very little to influence student achievement, then it is very likely these beliefs will be manifested in their practice.

—Donohoo (2017, p. 7)

Collective teacher efficacy (1.57 effect size) —Each stakeholder in a school has a strength. This influence is about bringing those individuals together to maximize that strength with a goal of fostering a stronger focus on learning.

—Dewitt (2017, p. 6)

By strengthening collective teacher efficacy, teachers will develop the resolve to persist against challenges and realize increased student results.

—Donohoo (2017, p. 36)

A Framework for the Preparation of Teachers of ELs to Teach Reading and Content in the Secondary Schools

The purpose of this chapter is to share the findings from the ExCELL research on ways to enhance professional development programs. It is the hope of the authors that this framework will assist school districts in the design and implementation of quality professional development programs centered on teaching literacy or biliteracy through social studies, science, math, and/or language arts domains.

Focusing on Quality Teachers for Reading in the Content Areas

The National Reading Panel (NRP, 2000) and the Reading Next researchers and policy makers were highly concerned with teacher education for reading. The NRP found preservice education focuses on changing teacher behavior without a concomitant focus on the outcomes of students who are eventually instructed by those teachers. This emphasis is also apparent in the field with the onslaught of "reading models" where the developers are quick to attribute student outcomes to their intervention and not the teachers. Although reading instruction involves four interacting factors—students, tasks, materials, and teachers—the NRP found research has rarely focused on teachers, instead emphasizing students, materials, and tasks. Therefore, teacher education and its impact on the teachers' and their students' learning has been largely ignored. Notwithstanding, current researchers are beginning to focus more on the role of the teacher and the whole school as the best vehicle to bring about effective student outcomes (Calderón & Slakk, 2017a; Donohoo, 2017; Hattie, 2015; Hattie & Yates, 2014). Collective efficacy, as described by these authors, can be applied to whole-school efforts to improve literacy for all students, plus ELs specifically.

For a long time, there has been a general scientific consensus among researchers and comprehensive research review panels that certain components are necessary for teaching basic reading skills (Learning First Alliance, 2000; National Reading Panel, 2000; Pacific Resources for Education and Learning, 2002; Slavin & Cheung, 2004; Snow, Burns & Griffin, 1998). This research has been incorporated into most reading initiatives in the primary grades. However, other efforts began looking at reading in secondary schools. In *Reading Next: A Vision for Action and Research in Middle and High School Literacy* (Biancarosa & Snow, 2004), and the 2010 Carnegie report *Reading in the Disciplines: The Challenges of Adolescent Literacy* (Lee & Spratley, 2010) attention was finally given to comprehension, learning while reading, reading content areas, and reading in the service of secondary or higher education, of employability, of citizenship.

Educators must figure out how to ensure that every student gets beyond the basic literacy skills of the early elementary grades, to the more challenging and more rewarding literacy of the middle and secondary school years. Inevitably, this will require, for many of those students, teaching them new literacy skills: how to read purposefully, select materials that are of interest, learn from those materials, figure out the meanings of unfamiliar words, integrate new information with information previously known, resolve conflicting content in different texts, differentiate fact from opinion, and recognize the perspective of the writer—in short, they must be taught how to comprehend (Biancarosa & Snow, 2004, p. 1).

Through the specific recommendation and funding from the Carnegie Corporation of New York, the ExC-ELL project was created to "figure out" how to design staff development programs for middle and high school teachers of language arts, English as a second language, social studies, science, and math that have one or more ELs in their classrooms. We have discussed in previous chapters the language, literacy, and content instructional components that resulted from our research and components testing. This chapter describes the process of professional development that was also empirically studied as it was implemented in middle and high schools across diverse schools and their diverse EL populations embedded in regular content classrooms.

The Process of Professional Development

The process for professional development described in this chapter has a long history of development. It was based on research and empirical studies. Early on, we realized that transforming professional knowledge into teaching habits requires time and a variety of professional activities (Learning First Alliance, 2000). Recognizing the link between professional development and successful educational change (Darling-Hammond & McLaughlin, 1995; Lieberman, 1995), and results-driven education (Sparks & Hirsh, 1997), we realized that quality teacher training had to be offered to teachers of ELs. For teachers to espouse new instructional strategies and effectively transfer all of that into the classroom, several components needed to be included in the design.

Teachers need theory, research, modeling or demonstrations of instructional methods, coaching during practice, and feedback to integrate instructional practices into their active teaching repertoire (Joyce & Showers, 1988). Therefore, the professional development was built on principles stemming from the research. We now see these principles in the most recent research (Hattie, 2012; Dewitt, 2017; Donohoo, 2017).

Guidelines of Training for Teachers and Administrators With ELs

- Teachers need presentations on current theory and research on language, literacy, and content integration.
- Experts need to model effective strategies for building word knowledge, comprehension, and writing for teaching English language learners.
- Teachers need time to practice and exchange ideas with peers after each segment or strategy at the workshops to inquire, reflect, and respond to new ideas if they are to embrace them.
- Experts provide low-risk practice sessions in the workshop setting where teachers practice teaching strategies in small teams.
- Experts provide opportunities for reading and teacher reflection through cooperative learning activities.
- Experts include as part of their workshop, explanations and demonstrations of peer coaching practices and collaborative work that promote the transfer of new teaching skills into the classroom (Joyce & Showers, 1988; Calderón, 1994b; Calderón, Minaya-Rowe, & Carreón, 2006).

When Bruce Joyce and Beverly Showers worked with our Multidistrict Trainer of Trainers Institutes in the early 1980s in California, they used the matrix shown in Figure 9.1 to illustrate the effect sizes for student outcomes contingent on the type of training teachers received. They explained that when lectures or theory is the only component presented to teachers, there is only minimal transfer into the classroom. The same occurs when the professional development provides only a set of isolated instructional strategies.

At the end of the school year, we can predict that approximately only 5% of the teachers will be using the new strategies. This 5% comprises teachers who figured out how to implement that research. Unfortunately, such a small number of teachers will have minimal impact on student outcomes. Sometimes they even give up when other teachers set out to discourage the "brave pioneers."

Why a Whole-School Approach to PD on EL Instruction

In many cases, it is only the ESL/ELD teacher who attends an inservice to learn about ELs. The impact on ELs is that same 5% a year later. On the other hand, when theory, demonstrations, practice, feedback, and coaching/collegial activities are integrated into a comprehensive staff development program, teachers transfer into the classroom, and positive student outcomes are the result.

Our whole-school approach finds that the more teachers attend the inservice, the more powerful the student results. A whole-school approach to professional development on knowing, supporting, and teaching ELs is the best way to achieve EL success, as well as success for all other students in the school. When the ExC-ELL model is implemented as a whole-school approach, huge student academic growth results. In fact, we can forecast for schools and districts what to expect with only ESL teachers or the one-and-done workshop for general education teachers in comparison to whole-school comprehensive professional development throughout the year.

Figure 9.1   Importance of Comprehensive Whole-School Professional Development

Type of Training Components	Level of Knowledge	Level of Skill	Transfer One Year Later	
			Teacher Use	Student Effect Size
Theory and Lecture	80%	5%	5%	0.01
Modeling and Demos	90–95%	50%	5%	0.03
Practice and Feedback	95–100%	80–90%	5%	0.39
Coaching and PLCs/ TLCs	95–100%	98–100%	75–95%	1.68

Joyce & Showers, 1981; Sharan & Hertz-Lazarowitz, 1982; Calderón, 1984, 2001, 2007, 2012; Calderón & Slakk, 2017.

Current Views of the Same Research

The research on the chart has been replicated throughout the years and has continued to yield similar effect sizes. Currently, researchers such as John Hattie (2015), Jenni Donohoo (2017), and Peter Dewitt (2017) espouse and elaborate on Bruce Joyce's framework. For example, John Hattie conducted hundreds of meta-analyses from various databases and identified "collective teacher efficacy" as having 1.57 effect size, the highest effect size for creating desired impact on students. Hattie (2015) states that "the greatest influence on student progression in learning is having highly expert, inspired and passionate teachers and school leaders working together to maximize the effect of their teaching on all students in their care" (p. 2).

Donohoo expands on collaborative efficacy, which includes coaching, self-reflection, feedback, and working with colleagues. She uses the Tschannen-Moran and Barr (2004, p. 190) definition of collaborative efficacy as the "collective self-perception that teachers in a given school make an educational difference to their students over and above the educational impact of their homes and communities." She emphasizes that fostering collaborative teacher efficacy should be at the forefront of a planned strategic effort in all schools and school districts.

All three authors add detail to the relationship between professional development, coaching, self-efficacy and what we call Teachers Learning Communities (Calderón, 1999) and expand on these principles focusing on teacher, school leaders, and system. For Dewitt, collaborative leadership in a school means that the administrator's role is to provide support, time, and resources for collective teacher efficacy to happen by

- Creating a positive school climate that puts a focus on learning
- Co-creating learner dispositions with teachers
- Co-constructing goals with staff for more productive teacher observations
- Co-constructing goals for faculty meetings to make them more like professional development (Dewitt, 2017, p. 54)

In our PD sessions for administrators, we integrate the following topics that will be expanded upon later in this chapter:

- Evaluating and selecting an effective professional development and support model
- Administrator professional development

- Supporting teachers and Teacher Learning Communities (TLCs)
- Setting implementation expectations with the whole school

Hattie also emphasizes that goal-oriented deliberate practice is necessary. When practice is accompanied by feedback and self-reflection/self-evaluation, teachers acquire automaticity. In our studies, we found that a minimum of 2 years is needed for teachers to practice, be supported and coached, reflect and refine, and work through the stages of learning, as shown in Figure 9.2.

Hattie and associates found that observation protocols are vital for coaching and self-evaluation. We created and began using the ExC-ELL Observation Protocol (EOP) from the beginning of the study in 2005 to collect implementation data. Since then, it has evolved into The WISEcard EOP (Walkthrough of Instructional Strategies via ExC-ELL), which helps the teachers, coaches, and school leaders support the teachers' learning. It gives them the type of data they all need to gauge the learning progressions of teachers and students. As principals use it, they themselves learn the intricacies of implementation

Figure 9.2   Year Professional Development Loop

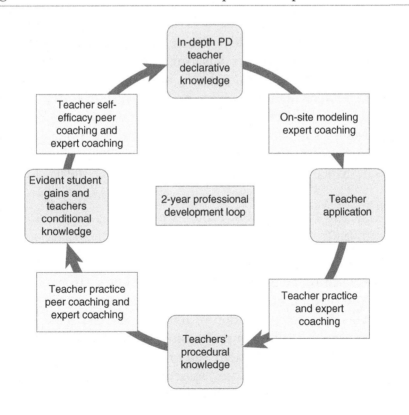

and what instruction for ELs and their peers should look like. Teachers use it as a self-reflection tool for improving lesson development and delivery. In conjunction with videotaping, the teachers share their reflections in their TLCs and invite feedback from peers.

Features of a Comprehensive Professional Development Model

3- to 5-Day Training on ExC-ELL Foundations: Expediting Reading Comprehension for English Language Learners and Low-Performing Readers Through Close Reading of Complex Texts in All Subject Areas

The professional development model focuses on the type of academic language and vocabulary that leads to close reading, reading comprehension of content and complex texts, and use in text-based writing. Performance assessments for gauging vocabulary, close reading for comprehension, and writing are integrated into the instruction and curriculum materials the teachers bring to the session.

2-Day Academy for Administrators and Site-Based Coaches

In addition to attending the 3- to 5-day sessions to learn and practice the instructional strategies with the teachers, administrators attend 2 more days. This academy is focused on how to support teachers through the implementation phases, how to observe, what shows evidence of implementation, how to give productive feedback, how to promote self- and collective efficacy plus collective planning of next steps to sustain the innovation. The principals, assistant principals, and coaches practice using the observation protocol by shadowing the ExC-ELL coaches when they come to their schools to coach the teachers.

2-Day Training on Reaching Newcomer/Refugee Students Institute

ExC-ELL strategies focus on Newcomers and SIFE students who need basic reading skills development and a strong foundation for close reading of complex texts. For this reason, the RIGOR program was developed (Calderón, 2007). In RIGOR, the ExC-ELL vocabulary, reading, and comprehension strategies are adapted to Newcomers, along with student self-efficacy and socio-emotional support strategies. Performance assessments for gauging vocabulary and close reading for comprehension and writing are integrated into the instruction and curriculum materials the teachers bring to the session. The teachers must have attended a 3-day Institute on the ExC-ELL Foundations.

Supporting ExC-ELL Implementation With On-Site Classroom Master Coaching

ExC-ELL coaches provide individualized in-class coaching and mentoring, focusing on implementation and adaptation of instructional strategies. Principals and coaches are invited to shadow the expert coaches.

Staff Development Models and Outcomes: What the Evidence Says

Another way of looking at the impact of a training design is to consider the differences between these two models:

Model A—Consists of a 5-day workshop on a new reading program conducted during the summer or at the beginning of the school year without follow-up support for teachers.

Model B—Consists of (1) a 3- to 5-day workshop with (2) multiday on-site in-class follow-up coaching for each component and TLC support for teachers, and (3) rigorous measures to determine level of implementation, teacher progress with new instructional strategies, and student language learning progressions on the way to stated academic goals and projected outcomes.

When we compare Model A and B, we see teachers remain at an initial level of knowledge and instructional skill without impact on students implementing Model A. On the other hand, Model B adds structured follow-up from an inservice through school-based Teachers Learning Communities and appropriate measures. In Model B, teachers can reach an expert level in even 1 year. What's more, the impact on their students becomes significant.

A backwards-planning approach to staff development designs enables one to focus on the student outcomes a school desires first. For instance, the first phase begins with vocabulary development as the desired outcome

> *Results-driven education and teacher-focused professional development needs to begin* by determining the things ELs need to know and be able to do; then, working backwards to the knowledge, skills, and attitudes required of educators if those student outcomes are to be realized.

before students can delve into reading comprehension. To measure such an outcome, the teachers' level of knowledge about preteaching vocabulary, teaching vocabulary during and after reading, before, during, and after writing; the quality of delivery; the frequency of use of those strategies; and the way they adapt them to ELs and other students, are all important to document, coach, and practice. This is what we refer to as *knowing the level of transfer from training into the classroom—how well, how often, and how effectively teachers use the new strategies in their own classrooms.*

Data Collection

Continuing with the vocabulary example, as the decisions are made for the staff development design, measures and instrumentation for data collection must also be determined. At the student level, measures should be connected to the staff development focus as much as possible. For a vocabulary intervention, pre- and posttests of vocabulary in each content area can be used for both experimental and control student cohorts to measure differences. The vocabulary subtest of a standardized test such as the Woodcock-Johnson can also be used to measure and compare both cohorts. If, as we know, vocabulary correlates with reading comprehension, then a test of reading comprehension can also be used. Student writing samples collected monthly are also good indicators of application, depth, and breadth of word knowledge in a subject.

Students Learn What Teachers Teach. Classroom observation instruments such as the WISEcard can help supervisors, coaches, and the teachers themselves gauge the progress of quality instruction. Video analysis, analysis of student work, and exchanges in TLCs are indicators of teachers' progress. The WISEcard also shows the creative contributions of each teacher and how students respond to that instruction.

Teachers Learn What Teacher Trainers Teach. Ways of measuring the effect of the staff development intervention are usually self-reporting evaluations, which basically tell us about the climate in the room, the food, and how they felt about a trainer or how they were feeling that day. Specificity needs to be built into the training evaluation to anticipate strong or weak outcomes and to redesign the training based on those weaknesses. Otherwise, we are shortchanging our teachers. Here are a few key indicator questions:

Figure 9.3   Relationship Between Training, Teacher, and Student Outcomes

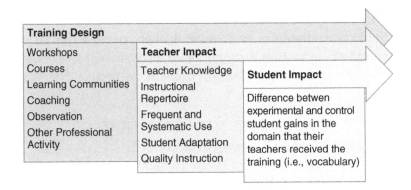

Data on the Relevance of the Training

1. Is the information being presented at the forefront of research-based knowledge? Is the information presented based upon recent research? Within the last 5 to 10 years? This is particularly important when it comes to EL instruction, since most presenters are still espousing theories/hypotheses that have never been proven by research.

2. Is the research accompanied with practical instructional strategies and techniques, or do teachers have to figure these out on their own? Do the strategies and techniques presented come with explicit steps and modeling?

3. What is the teacher interaction during those workshops? Are they excited as they participate in the demonstrations and practice? Are they expected to bring their own lessons on which to apply the newly learned strategies?

4. Do their questions reflect interest in implementation? Do their comments reflect excitement about trying them out and how applicable the strategies or techniques are to their ELs and their other students?

5. Is all this relevant to their students? Is it grade-level appropriate? Subject appropriate?

Transfer From Training

What happens after the workshop, institute, or in-school professional development is the most important phase of professional development. Does implementation start Day 1? Or does it get left to fade into the record as just another PD session? When participants return to the daily routines, this is the critical juncture of implementation; those daily routines need to be replaced by implementing as many of the new strategies as possible. Collective reflection in small groups and self-regulation through video analysis helps to begin the first phase of transfer into classroom implementation.

Micro-level Indicators for Classroom Implementation of Level of Impact

1. Do students learn five to ten new words during a class period and use them in oral summaries, conversations, writing, and comprehension tests?

2. Can teachers cite sources and explain the research-based instructional strategies they are using?

3. Does each teacher use the variety of evidence-based strategies for teaching vocabulary, reading, and writing integrated into their subject area?

4. Does the teacher invite other teachers to come and observe her or him teach for feedback and/or sharing strategies?

Duration of Training

A comprehensive staff development design would begin with an initial 5-day workshop/institute followed by another 10 days of lesson

Figure 9.4   Phase 1 Trajectory

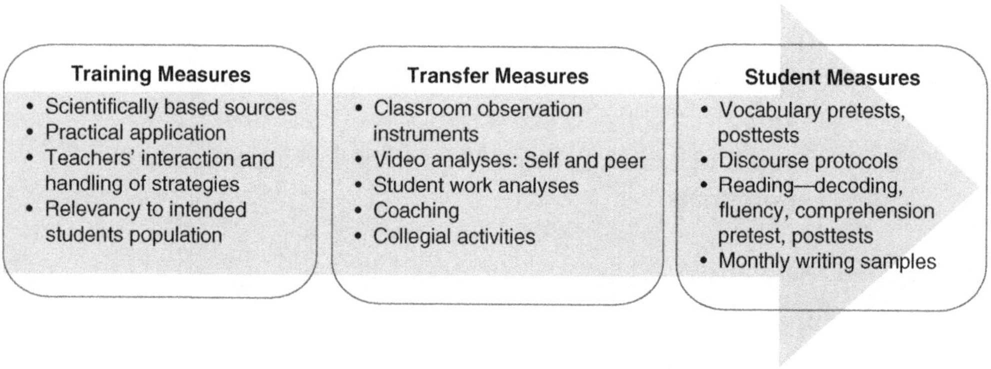

Training Measures
- Scientifically based sources
- Practical application
- Teachers' interaction and handling of strategies
- Relevancy to intended students population

Transfer Measures
- Classroom observation instruments
- Video analyses: Self and peer
- Student work analyses
- Coaching
- Collegial activities

Student Measures
- Vocabulary pretests, posttests
- Discourse protocols
- Reading—decoding, fluency, comprehension pretest, posttests
- Monthly writing samples

integration, parsing of texts, and collegial implementation support. When school starts, teacher practice in the classroom is accompanied with weekly 30-minute discussions with teacher colleagues in TLCs. In addition to the collegial learning at the school site, 2 or 3 additional days of inservice will be needed as refreshers and for building additional concepts, skills, and creative application. Some teachers will progress more rapidly with the integration of new learning into their teaching styles and student diversity. These quick learners can become peer coaches or mentors of others who need more confidence or technical assistance. While some teachers need to observe a strategy 5 or 6 times before they feel comfortable applying it, others will need more, but all will need an expectation of implementation. A one-size follow-up design does not fit all. If we are to individualize student learning, we must begin by individualizing teacher learning. Options we can offer teachers for their own professional growth after intensive workshops are

- Study groups
- Lesson development
- Peer coaching
- Action research (individual or with colleagues)
- Teacher portfolios
- Cultural histories/autobiography
- Train other teachers

Figure 9.5 Some Indicators of Implementation Success

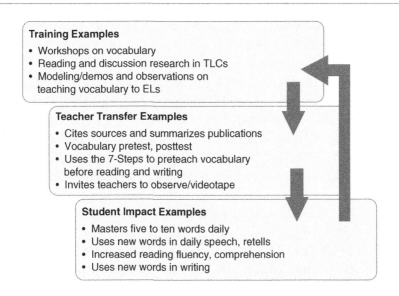

Weekly Collegial Study

According to Guskey (1998), Joyce and Showers (1988), and others, collegial activity is key for continuous learning on the job. Even after an inservice training, seasoned teachers need time to reflect and adapt new learning into their teaching. We can forecast the level of transfer based on the type of collegial activities teachers conduct on a weekly basis. We can easily predict that without collegial activity, teachers will begin to feel uncomfortable with an innovation after four weeks, and usually stop using the new instructional behaviors shortly thereafter. For this reason, it is critically important to build collegial skills and the mindset of continuous learning with peers before the inservice ends. We regularly suggest that the TLC building begins with these implementation and expectation notes. The following are just a few questions that will help spark the implementation process:

- What did *all* team members agree should be infused into the instruction in the classroom and school based on this professional development session?
- What are the first steps? By when?
- What more do you and your team need to be successful in transferring these new skills into the classroom?
- Do you yourself need more clarification on certain pieces? Who can you go to? One of your fellow participants? Do you have access to the trainer's contact information or trainer's website?

Answering these questions will help to focus what you've learned and come up with a plan and set of expectations for immediate implementation. Without such a plan and immediate action, teachers may well go back to their old familiar ways of teaching before the end of the school year (Calderón & Slakk, 2017a).

Our studies (Calderón, 1984; Calderón, 2005; Calderón, Minaya-Rowe, & Durán, 2005) have also documented the need to provide teachers with theory and practice on how to work in collegial teams. Because collegiality is difficult for many adults, the concept of collegiality needs to be established and practiced during all inservice workshops. It is also important to recognize that teachers add analytical, creative, and practical learning to their teaching and assessment methods. The bullet lists that follow show how teachers have used TLCs to further their and their peers' learning. Perhaps the most exciting side effect of TLCs is the one that TLC teachers receive from one another during critical times of change and difficulty, such as dealing with new assessments and standards.

As part of our inservice on literacy for ELs, teachers learn how to set up and run their own TLCs. The studies of TLCs in schools documented collegial activities of teachers that were different from their Professional Learning Communities (PLCs). Analysis of student data and discussions around that data typically happened in the PLCs. Other school or district mandates and logistics were discussed in PLCs, leaving little time to probe, discuss, or plan instruction. The teachers made the decision to establish TLCs where they met in small groups of their choice and focused more on building collective efficacy for classroom instruction.

Collegial Efficacy Practices in TLCs

- To model new strategies for each other; solve problems of student adaptation.
- Share teacher creativity through concrete products (lessons, curriculum, tests, etc.).
- Provide ongoing peer support, responsiveness, and assistance to all teachers.
- Share and discuss issues of classroom implementation, transfer from training, impact of teacher on student behavior and learning.
- Share ideas for new lessons or next steps.
- Schedule peer observations and coaching (Calderón, 1994b, 1999, 2000; Calderón & Minaya-Rowe, 2003).

The focus of TLCs varies across schools. Some ESL/ELD and content teachers spend once-a-month meeting time to analyze student products, interpret student data, and discuss implications for instructional improvement. Interpreting EL language proficiency test results can be most cumbersome and complex if it is not done in collaboration with others who have the same interests.

Student Performance Practices in TLCs

- Analyze student performance data.
- Reevaluate EL outcomes every 2 weeks.
- Work on instructional improvement based on the EL data.
- Get feedback on student writing and rubrics.
- Share lessons with the 12 components that worked with ELs and peers.
- Ask for suggestions on strategies.

> **TLCs**
>
> **Teachers' Learning Communities**
>
> Time, places, and spaces where teachers can collaboratively examine, question, develop, experiment, implement, evaluate, and create change.

Results from the students' pretests and posttests in the ExC-ELL project correlated with the level of TLC activities of teachers. When well implemented, TLCs can be places and spaces where teachers collaboratively examine, profoundly question, develop, experiment, implement, evaluate, and create exciting change. TLCs are opportunities for teachers to co-construct meaning to their craft and do whatever is necessary to help each other implement an innovation with fidelity. When studies are being conducted in their classrooms, teachers become co-researchers and eagerly contribute to the research and development of new programs. Their creative talents emerge as a new type of professional environment is established where they are respected for their expertise; they themselves invent and design ways that are more efficient and beneficial for them.

Summer Curriculum Institutes

A well-skilled worker is nothing without his or her proper tools. Teachers need carefully crafted lesson plans and yearlong curricula to accomplish their tasks. As part of a comprehensive staff development, teachers will need 2 to 4 weeks in the summer to integrate new reading strategies into their lessons, curriculum standards, and assessments. It is unreasonable to require teachers to do all this during the year as they are teaching and attempting to learn something new. This is the perfect time to set the expectation of a TLC and begin developing how the TLC will continue to function throughout the year.

Administrator Training for Teacher Support

Principals, curriculum coordinators, mentors, and other support personnel need to be well equipped to assist teachers in this difficult phase. Administrators must attend the workshops with the teachers. This is part of the professional development process for administrators, too. Leadership and support teams discuss the new information as well and share their views on what teachers should transfer to all the classrooms. This attention to the training shows teachers that the Leadership Team is part of the process, and when they see the administrators are attentive and actively participating, they have greater respect when the support teams coach and have suggestions (Calderón & Slakk, 2017b).

> Part of the administrator's job as the instructional leader is to provide resources, time for inservice training, and TLCs for job-embedded learning. Teachers cannot accomplish all this on their own time!

Later, administrators and support coaches attend a session exclusively for them where they learn and discuss how to build "teacher support mechanisms" and "help teachers recognize and capitalize on their strengths" through coaching and TLCs. However, this is only effective if they themselves have attended the initial inservice training. Forming a successful teacher development program will require building communities of practice where teachers, administrators, and students are learning all the time. As additional research on reading continues to emerge, pedagogy must adapt and readapt. As teachers are better prepared to teach reading, particularly to ELs, students' chances for learning to read will significantly increase.

Allocating time for staff development and time for TLCs is the first step toward success. The next step is to make sure teachers receive implementation visits from their administrators and coaches throughout the year. Yet, sustaining continuous learning and collegial activities will need a well-defined plan of implementation that needs to be revisited by teachers, coaches, and administrators 3 or 4 times a year. We have collected ideas from successful implementations from different parts of the country, which are synthesized below.

A Whole-School Approach to EL Success

We have had the pleasure of providing whole-school professional development with enlightened schools in New York City, Utah, Kauai, and Virginia. Some schools begin by training teachers from two or three subject areas; others one or two grade levels at a time. Loudoun County district office in Virginia chose half of the staff in a middle school and half of its feeder high school. When Margarita Calderón & Associates and George Washington University received one of the 5-year grants from the U.S. Department of Education's Office of English Language Acquisition, two other middle and high schools from Loudoun chose to participate in the whole-school approach. As we enter Year 2 of the grant, we continue preparing the other half of the teachers in the four schools, to coach the trained teachers, visit their TLCs when invited, and meet with principals to review the plan, adjust where necessary, and plan next steps. We co-constructed a list of "things to look for" every month. Donohoo would call this tool a shared vision protocol. (See our website www. ExC-ELL.com for the WISEcard EOP, which can be used as a monthly planning tool and checklist.)

When a new principal arrived at one of the middle schools, the other principals, assistant principals, teacher leaders, district specialists, and two of us from Margarita Calderón & Associates met to bring the principal up to date and address questions.

Principals have a huge challenge. Their role is to motivate the staff to keep on trying, to sustain high expectations for their students, and foster a closer look at instructional practices and mindsets. All this is on top of district mandates to implement certain initiatives that might even clash or contradict with evidence-based instruction for ELs. Accordingly, principals also need TLC. Special work sessions or debriefing sessions where all site administrators participate are just as important as TLCs for teachers. When the administrators from the implementing schools get together, they immediately start sharing, learning, and problem solving. They like to learn more about the subject from each other; not just what worked well, but also what to avoid. This is collaborative leadership at its best.

Bruce Joyce talked about the "implementation dip" that typically comes as early as October. He used to tell us that this dip is "natural, normal, and necessary" for growth, always using the bicycle analogy—how many times did you fall before you learned to ride it well? Therefore, we forecast for administrators that things will get worse around certain times before they get better. No matter how well everyone began the implementation, there are always those bumps or dips on the road that come up and must be overcome: (1) not enough time, (2) people reluctant to continue due to fear of failure, and (3) people who have certain perceptions about ELs and would like to see all of this go away. These are the things that school leaders should anticipate and seek collegial assistance when they start to occur. Just as teachers gain so much from collegial activity, so do administrators. Having multiple schools committed to whole-school participation makes the collective efficacy efforts stronger. They look out for one another. They move forward together: sometimes out of competition, because no one wants to get left behind. Competition is a good motivator to collaborate.

The *implementation dip* is also mentioned by Peter Dewitt (2017) as one that successful schools experience as they move forward with an innovation. He recommends planning for the dip in performance and confidence to address it. School faculties are still finding it difficult to talk about EL issues. Sometimes, there is a fear that the conversations

---

Sustaining Quality TLCs

✓ TLC activities need to be structured by specific agendas generated by teachers—the agenda should be flexible enough to allow teachers to meet their own emergent needs.

✓ TLC activities need to be brief—5 minutes for sharing successes, 5 minutes for problem solving, 10 minutes for instructional demos, 10 minutes for analyzing student work, 5 minutes for celebration.

✓ TLC activities need to be scheduled—as part of the school's calendar, and time has to be allocated during the workday.

---

will not remain "politically correct." Other times, it is due to the need for more information. This is an indication that more professional development is necessary to continue with those courageous conversations that will get them out of that dip.

A Corwin poster called the *Nottingham Poster* illustrates the learning challenge for students as they go from easy learning to interesting learning. Students are to begin with questions "What is ..."; "What if ..."; "What is the difference between ..." As they explore, they fall into the dip as they experience contradictions and confusions. However, they climb out of the pit by using certain strategies and at the top, they decide on ways they will use their new learning. We can use this parallel for those sticky conversations about EL success: What is their actual achievement status? How long has it been this way? Why? What is the difference between general education and EL instructional opportunities? The quality of instruction? What if all of us took ownership? As faculties explore, they will certainly fall into very uncomfortable realities. When they get past the dissonance, uncomfortable opposing biases, and seek further information and evidence-based strategies, they and their ELs will climb out of the pit and reach the desired pinnacle.

Implications for Implementation: Accountability and Quality

With poor English learner outcomes and increased emphasis on accountability by state and national policy makers, transforming teaching practices must go hand in hand with transforming professional development practices. Hard-nosed empirical studies and evaluation of staff development programs must be applied each time a workshop, an inservice, or the implementation of a new program is contemplated for EL achievement. We do not have a culture of rigorous professional development yet, much less an overabundance of evidence for what defines a high-quality teacher and what practices represent effective teaching for ELs. As the National Literacy Panel for Language Minority Children and Youth and the Carnegie Foundation Panel conclude in their findings, we can begin to make sure evidence guides all teacher training. For now, we have this empirically tested model, ExC-ELL and the accompanying inservices and classroom coaching models to begin to guide us.

Summary

✓ Any professional development program must be comprehensive and systematic.

✓ All teachers in secondary schools benefit from professional development programs focusing on academic language, reading, and writing in the content areas.

✓ TLCs are just as important as inservices, and sustain what teachers learn at an inservice.

✓ TLCs must be allocated quality time during the school week.

✓ TLCs need to be carefully crafted and sustained.

✓ There's a direct correlation between the quality and intensity of a professional development program and student outcomes for ELs.

10

Implementing ExC-ELL

A Principal's Perspective

This chapter provides one principal's insight and a few tools for school administrators, literacy coaches, content coaches, and district-level professional development teams on how to observe, reflect, and coach teachers implementing ExC-ELL using the train the trainer model.

Tarcia Gilliam-Parrish, EdD

Middle School Principal, Shelby County Public Schools, TN

Teacher Support Systems and Implementation

Teacher support systems and implementation plan are as important as the strategies themselves. English learners (ELs) are entering schools on every grade level every day of the school week. Instructional leaders are charged with providing a systematic approach to providing grade-level instruction in hopes of preparing students for state assessments and college entry exams.

As the Instructional Leader, the goals I establish must be clear: create opportunities for success for adults and students, analyze the data to inform instruction, and increase student college and career readiness. Our four focus areas, which are (1) creating a climate for learning, (2) access to rigorous content and quality of instruction, (3) provide targeted support and enrichment, (4) target support for struggling learners' skills that are specific to homework and practice, are partnered with parents and intentional professional learning opportunities for all educators.

Develop the Process

Building capacity is shared leadership and refers to development and support. It sustains itself through an inquiry cycle:

What is happening in the classroom?

What resources and tools are being implemented?

What do we know about student past performance and projected future progress?

What support can we provide for teachers, students, and parents?

Leadership is a link between leaders and followers with integrity. As the building level administrator, I lead the implementation process with integrity, intentional steps, and purposeful structures for all stakeholders. Leadership does not mean control. The moment we try to control others, we create an environment of acceptance.

English Learners face a dual challenge: acquiring the English language for basic communication and understanding academic content knowledge. It is necessary to reduce anxiety of the experience for many ELs by providing them high-interest books and resources to meet that dual challenge. ExC-ELL resources that support reading, listening, speaking, and writing ensure that ELs receive explicit instruction and practice with level-appropriate skills and strategies.

During the teaching process, we often ask the following questions: How do English Learners learn best? What instructional strategies are most effective for the English Language Learners? According to Dr. Calderón's research, the quality of the instruction may be more important than the language of the instruction when it comes to providing effective educational programs for ELs (Slavin, Madden, Calderón, Chamberlain, & Hennessy, 2009). Calderón defines high-quality instruction as strategic, systematic, and incrementally built on what students already know. She also says that making instruction explicit will boost English Learner comprehension and participation in learning. Dr. Calderón developed the ExC-ELL program to provide teachers with the 12 components that are essential for effective instruction. Many students struggle to make connections between what they are taught in the classroom and how those skills appear on high-stakes tests, especially when the tests have technology-enhanced items with which students don't have much experience.

The program was designed with all ELs receiving structured instruction in all content areas. Structured instruction in ExC-ELL means all instruction is delivered in English, but teachers use strategies to help meet students' linguistic needs, such as the explicit teaching of vocabulary, reading comprehension, and writing. In Shelby County (Tennessee), students either receive push-in or pull-out services to meet ESL/ELD/SPED requirements. Push-in means specialists or aids work with ELs within the mainstream classroom. Pull-out means ELs spend a portion of the day developing their English language skills with specialists, as required by law. Both general education and ESL/ELD teachers use the same strategies for their lesson delivery. Student understanding of new concepts may be enhanced through instruction that uses routines, embeds redundancy in lessons, provides explicit discussion of vocabulary and structure, and teaches students metacognitive skills (August & Hakuta, 1997). Although August and Hakuta do not specify reading instruction in their publication, these practices are used in the teaching of reading and writing in ExC-ELL.

Support Systems

At our school, the plan was to create a systematic system that would be sustainable throughout the year. We created a system of continuous learning among the adult learners with a "teachers train teachers" model. The goal was to build capacity within teacher leaders. The train the trainer model consists of the middle out approach. "Teachers train teachers" involves initially training a person who, in turn, trains other teachers within their discipline departments. Teachers who possess a higher capacity to intentionally lead training and follow-up coaching at the school are selected. The school-level leader/administrator and one teacher from every content and specialty area are involved: one math, science, social studies, English language arts, special education, and ESL/ELD teacher.

After the initial training, those trained in the ExC-ELL vocabulary strategy meet as an ExC-ELL team to discuss strategies presented during the initial training. During the meeting, the protocol is developed for schoolwide implementation deciding on who will lead the faculty and staff training, what portions will be delivered, and which strategies will be shelved for the next presentation. In the meantime, the ExC-ELL Master Coaches conduct coaching visits. The school-site trainers shadow the ExC-ELL Master Coaches and conduct informal classroom visits. Our school-based trainers visit each other's classes for a quick 10-minute visit, which is immediately followed by a feedback session to discuss specific findings. The informal classroom observers use the same WISEcard that the ExC-ELL Master Coaches use because mimicking the process works for all new strategies. After a few weeks, the lead team is trained on *reading*. The follow-up at the school repeats the same cycle of support as that described for the *vocabulary phase*. Subsequently, the team is trained on *writing*, and the cycle of school-based collegial learning takes place.

The initially trained group visits schoolwide classrooms after the whole group presentation for staff and faculty. They mimic the process while they observe the delivery of vocabulary strategy using the WISEcard. After the observation, it is essential that they provide immediate feedback. As a group, they discuss what is observed. Planning for the visit includes having teachers sign up for informal observation, while attending the district-level training and school-level training. A no-surprises approach works best for effective implementation. The WISEcard information is shared schoolwide. Expectation and simplification of the process provides an opportunity to grow in all aspects of the implementations.

During the ExC-ELL Master Coaches' visits, school-level instructional leaders accompany the team throughout the day. This provides a snapshot of the visitor's views of your schoolwide implementation. The feedback received from the visitor is shared with the staff. It is important to trust that they are doing the tough work, but verify that the work is being done effectively. Inspect what you expect! In other words, to trust the growth process, it is important to monitor the planning process. During all levels of implementation, we effectively mentor, develop, and improve the performance of others in such a manner that the entire experience becomes contagious and changes the quality of life for others.

- *Intentional support around implementation of the curriculum.* We created multiple ways for this to be accomplished including having two weekly PLCs with one focusing on planning for the ExC-ELL strategy and integration curriculum and the other focusing on analyzing and using data. We selected priorities for lesson planning and providing feedback around those rotating strategies. In addition, we talked about the importance of collaborative planning time for the content team and made sure all teachers were signed up for next round of ExC-ELL PD.

- Coaches support and collaborate with Instructional Leadership Team (ILT). We discussed the need to continue to focus on alignment and collaboration between coaches, administrative members, and ILT content leaders.
- During each coaching conversation, it was an absolute pleasure to work with teachers. Each teacher greatly appreciated the support the ExC-ELL consultants and their school training team gave throughout the year. This continued training created a culture of learning and growth and instilled a continuous learning spirit at our school.

Implementation of ExC-ELL Tips

Strategies

- ✓ Determine the biggest challenges and long-term implementation of the strategies.
- ✓ Eliminate the obstacles and include everyone. Share the benefits for students when they receive systematic instruction in vocabulary, reading, and writing.

Alignment

- ✓ What is necessary to gain support from even reluctant folks for the new program?
- ✓ Cultivate a winning culture—all things are possible to those that are trained.

Plan

- ✓ Determine key milestones needed to complete the plan and implement the program.
- ✓ Continue with team development—School-level leader, content teachers, specialty areas (Special Education, ESL/ELD, Creative Learning in a Unique Environment (CLUE/Gifted) students.

Implementation

- ✓ What resources are necessary?
- ✓ Build your momentum and sustain it.

✓ Build strengthen in your muscles—actual initial roll out of the program.

✓ Discuss long-term plan with groups.

✓ Execute, revise, refocus, and redefine.

✓ Review and evaluate.

✓ Determine ways to measure program success.

✓ Make sure all next steps are time bound and measurable.

✓ Use evaluations connected to learning teams to learn and grow.

✓ Use highly effective feedback.

✓ Collaborate to develop implementation goals.

✓ Determine specific strategies based on identified areas for growth with clear "Look-Fors" and timelines for regular check-ins.

✓ Developing effective and ongoing feedback takes practice, practice, practice.

In response to the 2015 Every Student Succeeds Act (ESSA), states have started to adopt new standards and assessment systems designed to ensure that all students are ready for college and careers. Rather than focusing on basic procedural knowledge, these new standards and assessment systems require students to demonstrate complex higher-order cognitive skills such as the ability to analyze, synthesize, compare, connect, critique, and hypothesize. They also gain the ability to apply knowledge to new contexts. Teachers face the challenging goal of building student academic language, content knowledge and higher-order thinking skills, while also preparing students to perform on high-stakes tests. ExC-ELL strategies help meet these needs by translating the best research in EL learning strategies, pedagogy, and instructional design. By combining adaptive instructional strategies, specific differentiated teacher feedback, strategic coaching, and detailed follow-up, ExC-ELL empowers students with the critical knowledge, higher-order thinking skills, and deeper learning competencies needed for success. To make these successes available to the students, we must first provide the teachers the opportunity to fully understand the need and build their capacity on how to address them. The systemic approach to implementing the necessary teacher skills are outlined as follows:

- Principals attend ExC-ELL professional development session.
- A schoolwide implementation plan is developed.
- Principals and content teacher leaders attend the off-campus training.
- Content Lead Teachers lead their teams through the same training.

- An implementation schedule of the methodology is developed. (We started with vocabulary implementation via an observation schedule for peer observations.)
- Teachers are given immediate feedback by ExC-ELL expert coaches and school-site Lead Teachers.

Implementing Vocabulary/Academic Language. ExC-ELL trainers come and observe teachers' implementation of vocabulary, reading, and writing strategies. Trainers give immediate feedback to teachers. During our feedback conversations, we discuss the support that took place, the actual strategy, and review ways of improving our process and approach. Principal, content leaders, and ExC-ELL trainers participate in the feedback session. Afterwards, the discussion notes and feedback are shared with the entire staff.

Throughout the year, we have seen growth in teachers as they began to trust that this support was being given for their benefit. We expect that more growth will take place rapidly over the next year because we have established a solid foundation and created a teacher-learning environment that relies on feedback and focuses on a growth mindset.

As we move forward into the upcoming school year, we are discussing how we envision the next steps and the elements we consider to be essential. We developed intentional support around implementation of the curriculum. We discussed multiple ways that this might be accomplished during our weekly PLCs. We also talked about selecting priorities for lesson planning and providing feedback around those rotating priorities. Much emphasis should be placed on the importance of collaborative planning time for the teaching teams and coaching support and collaboration with ILT.

Implementing Content-Based Reading Comprehension. During the Reading strategy implementation, our school-level administrators and teacher leaders met after the district-level training. We discussed focus strategies that we would share with the faculty and implement schoolwide. We started with partner reading with summarization. Lead teachers and administrators introduced the staff to the next strategy. We practiced the partner read strategy as an ILT before taking it to the staff and walked them through the process as they practiced it with each other before implementing it in their classroom. We allowed teachers to sign up for peer observation time and feedback sessions. During peer observations, teachers only observed the partner reading strategy. During the feedback session, observers only discussed the partner reading strategy. This laser-like focus allowed teachers to improve on one strategy at a time. The feedback we received from teachers about the process emphasized their appreciation for being able to participate in focused peer observations, receiving immediate feedback, and the opportunity to have observers from different levels (school-level, district-level, and ExC-ELL trainers). Teachers stated students' vocabulary and reading enjoyment increased with partner reading. Students stated that the reading was made easier in teams of two or three (teams of three include a Newcomer). Students also shared that they were more interested and engaged in reading during all classrooms.

For every school-level observation session and teacher learning conferences, teachers were given the weekly schedule for the ExC-ELL Coaching sessions. Teachers signed up for observation times to ensure we would observe the strategy being implemented. For each observation, the observing team was given two copies of the WISE-card protocol to be used during the observation. A building-level administrator or team leader observed alongside the ExC-ELL team and listened during the coaching session that followed.

ExC-ELL has increased collaboration during the whole-school implementation. All teachers collaborated during content curriculum meetings on words and strategies to use and to streamline the process and flow of a lesson. During Peer- and Self-Observations, all teachers newly and previously trained in ExC-ELL benefited from using the WISEcard for personal and collegial observations of implementations. The Science and Math staff are placed in pairs each one with a colleague who has been trained in ExC-ELL to help those departments to see the benefits of using ExC-ELL across all curriculum, classrooms, and lessons at our middle school.

Implementing Content-Based Writing. Schoolwide implementation of writing was difficult. To increase the implementation of the strategies with fidelity, more peer coaching was necessary. Teachers also had to be convinced that organized and effective teaching of writing helped students learn to write while learning content. We created a common writing language. Prior to conducting the informal classroom observations of explicit instruction, we observed implicit teaching of writing.

Bringing It All Together. We created a survey regarding the school-level professional development sessions, how confident they felt with using the ExC-ELL vocabulary strategies, and where they needed additional practice or support. Our results showed that the following elements were present:

- Academic vocabulary (i.e., Tier 1, 2, and 3 words) was being implemented.
- Language (i.e., rich discussions, argumentative discourse, questions, answers) was being implemented.
- Reading (i.e., text complexity, reading closely for different purposes) was being implemented.
- Writing from sources (i.e., texts students are reading; writing in all subject areas); needed more content-based professional learning opportunities.
- Building knowledge in the disciplines (i.e., by teaching reading, vocabulary, and writing in math, science, social studies, and language arts); needed more learning opportunities.

We invited school-based ExC-ELL trained leaders to lead school-level professional learning to reiterate the focus area of writing in the content areas. During the session, we began using an electronic ExC-ELL Lesson Integration Tool to give teachers the option of creating ExC-ELL lessons digitally. During the meetings, the math and science teams discussed how to implement and infuse ExC-ELL strategies in math and science classrooms. Among the questions were how to implement reading and writing into the lessons so that students find the value of reading in each curriculum or writing in a subject such as math. After the meetings, all teachers worked extensively to infuse all aspects of ExC-ELL into their lessons and to have 100% participation.

During our next classroom observations of writing strategies, we observed the implementation of the teacher selected strategy, a variation of R.A.F.T. coupled with Ratiocination and Cut-n-Grow for revising and editing. Teachers explored more ways to preteach Tier 2 words, partner read, and summarize, while allowing students to formulate own questions. We observed the students reviewing as a class using the Numbered Heads strategy before beginning the writing process. During the feedback session, we discussed the flow and process for Partner Reading/Summarizing. We shared the Teacher Think-Aloud strategy to hook the reader. We determined that using a few short sentences orally is a good beginning for student summarization. Our observation also concluded that students benefit from having grammar, structure, features, or objectives modeled by the teacher. We modeled a short teacher Think-Aloud that moves students straight into the Partner Reading/Summarizing. For longer texts or for higher-level students, silent Paired Reading/Summarizing is also a configuration that supported accountability

As the building level administrator, I certainly know and understand how busy a principal's schedule can be, but also know the power of a visible principal that participates in the professional development and coaching provided to teachers. The principal's participation in this process does not only make a powerful statement about the administrator's commitment to improving the learning environment, but it also gives the administrator an understanding of what to expect during informal observations.

About Dr. Gilliam-Parrish

Tarcia Gilliam-Parrish, a native of Memphis, Tennessee, is a school administrator in the Shelby County Schools system, one of the largest urban districts in the United States.

She serves on several educational boards such as Tennessee Association for Supervision and Curriculum Development (TASCD) and has presented at the local, state, and national levels. She has been an instructional school leader for over a decade, and in the past 2 years, she has successfully implemented the *Expediting Reading Comprehension for English Language Learners* (ExC-ELL) model. The model focuses on professional development targeting science, social studies, math, and language arts teachers in a middle school with a student body demographics of 64% Hispanic.

She has published articles, chapters, and teacher-training materials. She is married to Lawrence Parrish and is mother to four daughters: Iesha and Teanna Gilliam, Shania Harmon, and Audrey Parrish.

References

Armbruster, B. B., Anderson, T. H., & Ostertag, J. (1987). Improving content-area reading using instructional graphics. *Reading Research Quarterly, 26* (4), 393–416.

August, D., Calderón, M., & Carlo, M. (2001). Transfer of reading skills from Spanish to English: A study of young learners. *National Association for Bilingual Education Journal, 24*(4), 11–42.

August, D., Calderón, M., & Carlo, M. (2002). *Transfer of reading skills from Spanish to English: A study of young learners.* Report ED-98-CO-0071 to the Office of Bilingual Education and Minority Languages Affairs, U.S. Department of Education.

August, D., Carlo, M., Calderon, M., & Proctor, P. (2005, Spring). Development of literacy in Spanish-speaking English-language learners: Findings from a longitudinal study of elementary school children. *The International Dyslexia Association, 31*(2), 17–19.

August, D., & Hakuta, K. (1997). *Improving schooling for language-minority children: A research agenda.* Washington, DC: National Research Council.

August, D., & Shanahan, T. (Eds.). (2006). Developing literacy in second language learners. *Report of the National Literacy Panel on Language Minority Children and Youth.* Mahwah, NJ: Lawrence Erlbaum.

August, D., & Shanahan, T. (Eds.). (2008). Developing reading and writing in second-language learners: Lessons from the report of the National Literacy Panel on Language Minority Children and Youth. New York, NY: Routledge.

Beck, I. L., & McKeown, M. G. (1991). Conditions of vocabulary acquisition. In R. Barr, M. Kamil, P. Mosenthal, & P. D. Pearson (Eds.), *Handbook of reading research* (Vol. 2, pp. 787–814). White Plains, NY: Longman.

Beck, I. L., McKeown, M. G., & Kucan, L. (2002). *Bringing words to life.* New York, NY: Guilford Press.

Bialystok, E., & Hakuta, K. (1994). *In other words: The science and psychology of second-language acquisition.* New York, NY: Basic Books.

Biancarosa, G., & Snow, C. E. (2004). *Reading next: A vision for action and research in middle and high school literacy: A report from Carnegie Corporation of New York.* Washington, DC: Alliance for Excellent Education.

Blachowicz, C. L. Z., & Fisher, P. (2000). Vocabulary instruction. In M. L. Kamil, P. B. Mosenthal, P. D. Pearson, & R. Barr (Eds.), *Handbook of reading research* (Vol. 3, pp. 503–523). Mahwah, NJ: Lawrence Erlbaum.

Boscolo, P., & Mason, L. (2001). Writing to learn, writing to transfer. In P. Tynjala, L. Mason, & K. Lonka (Eds.), *Writing as a learning tool* (pp. 83–104). Dordrecht, The Netherlands: Kluwer Academic.

Bromley, K., Irwin-DeVitis, L., & Modlo, M. (1995). *Graphic organizers: Visual strategies for active learning.* New York, NY: Scholastic Professional Books.

Brown, A. L., & Day, J. D. (1983). Macrorules for summarizing texts: The development of expertise. *Journal of Verbal Learning and Verbal Behavior, 22*(1), 1–14.

Calderón, M. (1984). *Training bilingual trainers: An ethnographic study of coaching and its impact on the transfer of training.* Doctoral dissertation, in Dissertation Abstracts and Claremont Graduate School/San Diego State University, 1984.

Calderón, M. (1994a). Cooperative learning for bilingual settings. In R. Rodriguez, N. Ramos, & J. Ruiz-Escalante (eds.) *Compendium of readings in bilingual education: Issues and practices.* San Antonio, TX: Texas Association for Bilingual Education.

Calderón, M. (1994b). Mentoring, peer support, and support systems for first-year minority/bilingual teachers. In R. A. DeVillar; C. J. Faltis, & J. P. Cummins (Eds.), *Cultural diversity in schools: From rhetoric to practice* (pp. 117–141). Albany, NY: State University of New York Press.

Calderón, M. (1999). Teachers Learning Communities for cooperation in diverse settings. In M. Calderón & R. E. Slavin (Eds.), *Building community through cooperative learning* [Special issue]. *Theory into Practice, 38*(2), 94–99.

Calderón, M. (November/December, 2000) Teachers' learning communities for highly diverse classrooms. *National Association for Bilingual Education Journal, 24*(2) 33–34.

Calderón, M. (2001). Curricula and methodologies used to teach Spanish-speaking limited English proficient students to read English. In R. E. Slavin & M. Calderón (Eds.), *Effective programs for Latino students* (pp. 251–305). Mahwah, NJ: Lawrence Erlbaum.

Calderón, M. (2005). Training teachers on effective literacy instruction for English language learners. In K. Telles & W. Hersh (Eds.), *Training teachers of language minority students.* Mahwah, NJ: Lawrence Erlbaum.

Calderón, M. E. (2007). *RIGOR! Reading Instructional Goals for Older Readers: Reading program for 6th–12th students with interrupted formal education.* New York, NY: Benchmark Education Co.

Calderón, M. E. (Ed.) (2012). *Breaking through: Effective instruction & assessment for reaching English learners. An anthology.* Indianapolis, IN: Solution Tree.

Calderón, M. E., August, D., Slavin, R. E., Duran, D., Madden, N., & Cheung, A. (2005). Bringing words to life in classrooms with English language learners. In E. H. Hiebert & M. L. Kamil (Eds.), *Teaching and learning vocabulary: Bringing research to practice* (pp. 115–136). Mahwah, NJ: Lawrence Erlbaum.

Calderón, M. E., & Carreón, A. (1994). Educators and students use cooperative learning to become biliterate and bilingual. *Cooperative Learning, 14* (3), 6–9.

Calderón, M. E., Hertz-Lazarowitz, R., & Slavin, R. E. (1998). Effects of bilingual cooperative integrated reading and composition on students making the transition from Spanish to English reading. *The Elementary School Journal, 99*(2), 153–165.

Calderón, M. E., & Minaya-Rowe, L. (2003). *Designing and implementing two-way bilingual programs: A step-by-step guide for administrators, teachers, and parents.* Thousand Oaks, CA: Corwin.

Calderón, M. E., Minaya-Rowe, L., & Carreón, A. (2006). *ExC-ELL: Expediting comprehension for English language learners: Teachers' manual.* Washington, DC: Margarita Calderón & Associates.

Calderón, M. E., Minaya-Rowe, L., & Durán, D. (2005). *Expediting comprehension to English language learners (ExC-ELL): Report to the Carnegie Foundation.* New York, NY: Carnegie Corporation of New York.

Calderón, M. E., & S. Slakk (2017a). *Promises fulfilled: A leader's guide for supporting English learners.* Bloomington, IN: Solution Tree.

Calderón, M. E. & S. Slakk (2017b). Taking the holistic approach! *Language Magazine.* Retrieved from http://languagemagazine.com/2017/03/taking-holistic-approach/

Calderón, M. E., Slakk, S., Carreón, A., & Peyton, J. (2017). *ExC-ELL: Expediting comprehension for English language learners* (3rd ed.). Washington, DC: Margarita Calderon & Associates Press.

Calderón, M. E., Slavin, R. E., & M. Sánchez. (2011). Effective instruction for English language learners. In M. Tienda & R. Haskins (Eds.). *The future of immigrant children* (pp. 103–128). Washington, DC: Brookings Institute/Princeton University.

Calderón, M. E., & Soto, I. (2017). *Academic language mastery: Vocabulary in context.* Thousand Oaks, CA: Corwin.

Carlo, M. S., August, D., & Snow, C. E. (2005). Sustained vocabulary-learning strategy instruction for English language learners. In E. H. Hiebert & M. L. Kamil (Eds.), *Teaching and learning vocabulary: Bringing research to practice* (pp. 137–154). Mahwah, NJ: Lawrence Erlbaum.

Chamot, A. U., & O'Malley, J. M. (1994). *The CALLA handbook: Implementing the cognitive academic language learning approach.* New York, NY: Addison-Wesley.

Cummins, J. (1984). *Bilingualism and special education: Issues in assessment and pedagogy.* London: Multilingual Matters.

Cunningham, A. E., & Stanovich, K. E. (1998). What reading does for the mind. *American Educator*, Spring-Summer, 8–17.

Dansereau, D. F. (1988). Cooperative learning strategies. In C. E. Weinstein, E. T. Goetz, & P. A. Alexander (Eds.), *Learning and study strategies: Issues in assessment, instruction, and evaluation* (pp. 103–120). Orlando, FL: Academic Press.

Darling-Hammond, L. (1998). Teacher learning that supports student learning. *Educational Leadership, 55*(5), 6–11.

Darling-Hammond, L., & McLaughlin, M. W. (1995). Policies that support professional development in an era of reform. *Phi Delta Kappan, 76*(8), 597–604.

Darling-Hammond, L., & Sykes, G. (2003). Wanted: A national teacher supply policy for education: The right way to meet the "highly qualified teacher" challenge. *Educational Policy Analysis Archives, 11*(33). Retrieved from http://epaa.asu.edu/epaa/v11n33/

Davey, B., & McBride, S. (1986). Effects of question generating training on reading comprehension. *Journal of Educational Psychology, 78*(4), 256–262.

Dewitt, P. M. (2017). *Collaborative leadership: Six influences that matter most.* Thousand Oaks, CA: Corwin.

Donohoo, J. (2017). *Collective efficacy: How educators' beliefs impact student learning.* Thousand Oaks, CA: Corwin.

Dowhower, S. L. (1987). Effects of repeated reading on second-grade transitional readers' fluency and comprehension. *Reading Research Quarterly, 22,* 389–406.

Duschl, R. A. (2007). Quality argumentation and epistemic criteria. In S. Erduran and M. P. Jimenez-Aleixandre (Eds.), *Argumentation in science education.* New York, NY: Springer.

Echevarria, J., & Graves, A. (1998). *Sheltered content instruction: Teaching students with diverse abilities.* Boston, MA: Allyn & Bacon.

Echevarria, J., Vogt, M. E., & Short, D. J. (2000). *Making content comprehensible for English language learners: The SIOP model.* Boston, MA: Allyn & Bacon.

Eldredge, J. L. (1990). Increasing the performance of poor readers in the third grade with a group-assisted strategy. *Journal of Educational Research, 84,* 69–77.

Fantuzzo, J. W., Polite, K., & Grayson, N. (1990). An evaluation of reciprocal peer tutoring across elementary school settings. *Journal of School Psychology, 28,* 309–323.

Fillmore, L. W. & Snow, C. E. (2002) What teachers need to know about language. In C. T. Adger, C. E. Snow, & D. Christian (Eds.), *What teachers need to know about language.* Washington, DC: Center for Applied Linguistics and Delta Systems.

Fitzgerald, J. (1995). English-as-a-second-language reading instruction in the United States: A research review. *Journal of Reading Behavior, 27* (2), 115–152.

Flower, L., & Hayes, J. (1980). The dynamics of composing: Making plans and juggling constraints. In L. Gregg and E. Steinberg (Eds.), *Cognitive processes in writing.* Hillsdale, NJ: Lawrence Erlbaum.

Foorman, B. R., & Mehta, P. (2002, November). *Definitions of fluency: Conceptual and methodological challenges.* PowerPoint presentation at A Focus on Fluency Forum, San Francisco, CA.

García, G. E. (2000). Bilingual children's reading. In M. L. Kamil, P. B. Mosenthal, P. D. Pearson, & R. Barr (Eds.), *Handbook of reading research* (Vol. 3, pp. 813–834). Mahwah, NJ: Lawrence Erlbaum.

Gillespie, A., & Graham, S.. (2011, Winter). Evidence-based practices for teaching writing. In R. Slavin (Ed.), *Better: Evidence-based education.* Cambridge, England: www.bestevidence.org/better

Goldenberg, C. (1992/1993). Instructional conversations: Promoting comprehension through discussion. *The Reading Teacher, 46,* 316–326.

Gottlieb, M. (2006). *Assessing English language learners. Bridges from language proficiency to academic achievement.* Thousand Oaks, CA: Corwin.

Graham, S., & Hebert, M. A. (2010). *Writing to read: Evidence for how writing can improve reading.* A Carnegie Corporation Time to Act report. Washington, DC: Alliance for Excellent Education.

Graves, M., August, D., & Carlo, M. (2011, Winter). Teaching 50,000 words. *Better: Evidence-based education, 3*(2), 6–7.

Guskey, T. (1998). Follow-up is key, but it's often forgotten. *Journal of Staff Development, 19*(2), 7–8.

Hattie, J.A.C. (2015). *What doesn't work in education: The politics of distraction.* London, England: Pearson.

Hattie, J.A.C., & Yates, G. (2014). *Visible learning and the science of how we learn.* New York, NY: Routledge.

Idol, L. (1987). Group story mapping: A comprehension strategy for both skilled and unskilled readers. *Journal of Learning Disabilities, 20*(4), 196–205.

Idol, L., & Croll, V. J. (1987). Story-mapping training as a means of improving reading comprehension. *Learning Disability Quarterly, 10*(3), 214–229.

Joyce, B., & Showers, B. (1988). *Student achievement through staff development.* New York, NY: Longman.

Juel, C. (1988). Learning to read and write: A longitudinal study of 54 children from first through fourth grades. *Journal of Educational Psychology, 80,* 437–447.

Kamil, M. L. (2005, June). *Review of key findings of NCLB legislation and research.* PowerPoint presentation, PREL Focus on Professional Development in Early Reading Forum, Honolulu.

Kenney, J. M., Hancewicz, E., Heuer, L., Metsisto, D., & Tuttle, C. L. (2005). *Literacy strategies for improving mathematics instruction.* Arlington, VA: ASCD.

King, A. (1994). Guiding knowledge construction in the classroom: Effects of teaching children how to question and explain. *American Educational Research Journal, 31*(2), 338–368.

King, M., Fagan, B., Bratt, T., & Baer, R. (1987). ESL and social studies integration. In J. Crandall (Ed.), *ESL through content area instruction: Mathematics, science, social studies* (pp. 89–119). Arlington, VA: Center for Applied Linguistics.

Klein, A. (2016, December). Final ESSA rules flesh out accountability, testing details. *Education Week.* December 13. http://www.edweek.org/ew/articles/2016/12/13/

Klingner, J. K., & Vaughn, S. (1998). Using collaborative strategic reading. *Teaching Exceptional Children, 30*(6), 32–37.

Koskinen, P. S., & Blum, I. H. (1986). Paired repeated reading: A classroom strategy for developing fluent reading. *The Reading Teacher, 40,* 70–75.

Krashen, S. D. (1981). Bilingual education and second language acquisition theory. In California State Department of Education (Ed.), *Schooling and language minority students: A theoretical framework* (pp. 51–82). Los Angeles, CA: Evaluation, Dissemination, and Assessment Center.

Krashen, S. D. (1982). *Principles and practice in second language acquisition.* Oxford, UK: Pergamon.

Learning First Alliance. (2000). *Every child reading: A professional development guide.* Baltimore, MD: Association for Supervision and Curriculum Development.

Lee, C. D., & Spratley, A. (2010). *Reading in the disciplines: The challenges of adolescent literacy.* New York, NY: Carnegie Corporation of New York.

Leos, K. (2006, June). Introductory remarks at the SIFE Share Fair. New York City Department of Education, Office of English Language Learners, New York City.

Lieberman, A. (1995). Practices that support teacher development. *Phi Delta Kappan, 76*(8), 591–596.

Malone, L. D., & Mastropieri, M. A. (1992). Reading comprehension instruction: Summarization and self-monitoring training for students with learning disabilities. *Exceptional Children, 58,* 270–279.

McKenna, M. C., & Robinson, R. D. (1990). Content literacy: A definition and implications. *Journal of Reading, 34,* 184–186.

Meloth, M. S., & Deering, P. D. (1992). The effects of two cooperative conditions on peer group discussions, reading comprehension, and metacognition. *Contemporary Educational Psychology, 17,* 175–193.

Meloth, M. S., & Deering, P. D. (1994). Task talk and task awareness under different cooperative learning conditions. *American Educational Research Journal, 31*(1), 138–165.

Menon, S., & Hiebert, E. H. (2003, April). *A comparison of first graders' reading acquisition with little books and literature anthologies.* Paper presented at the annual meeting of the American Educational Research Association, Chicago, IL.

Moats, L. (2017). A video interview with Louisa Moats. Retrieved from http://www.readingrockets.org/webcasts/3001#writing

Nagy, W. E., & Anderson, R. C. (1984). How many words are there in printed school English? *Reading Research Quarterly, 19* (3), 304–330.

National Academies of Sciences, Engineering, and Medicine. (2017). *Promoting the educational success of children and youth learning English: Promising futures.* Washington, DC: The National Academies Press.

National Commission on Writing. (2006). Writing and school reform: The neglected R. Retrieved from www.collegeboard.com.

National Commission on Writing. (2016). Study: Poor writing skills are costing business billions. Retrieved from https://www.inc.com/kaleigh-moore/study-poor-writing-skills-are-costing-businesses-billions.html

National Reading Panel. (2000). *Teaching children to read: An evidence-based assessment of the scientific research literature on reading and its implications for reading instruction.* Rockville, MD: National Institute of Child Health and Human Development.

Neuman, S. (2017). Discussion about writing. A video interview with Susan Neuman. Retrieved from http://www.readingrockets.org/webcasts/3001#writing

Newkirk, T. (March 2010). The case for slow reading. In *Reading to Learn. Educational Leadership, 67*(6), 6–11.

Olshavsky, J. E. (1976–1977). Reading as problem solving: An investigation of strategies. *Reading Research Quarterly, 12*(4), 654–764.

Osborn, J., Lehr, F., & Heibert, E. H. (2003). *A focus on fluency.* Monograph published by Pacific Resources for Education and Learning. Retrieved from http://www.prel.org/programs/rel/rel.asp

Pacific Resources for Education and Learning. (2002). *Readings on fluency for "A focus on fluency forum."* Honolulu, HI: Author.

Padrón, Y. N. (1992). The effect of strategy instruction on bilingual students' cognitive strategy use in reading. *Bilingual Research Journal, 16* (3&4), 35–52.

Padrón, Y. N., & Waxman, H. C. (1988). The effect of ESL students' perceptions of their cognitive reading strategies on reading achievement. *TESOL Quarterly, 22,* 146–150.

Palincsar, A. S. (1986). Reciprocal teaching. In *Teaching reading as thinking.* Oak Brook, IL: North Central Regional Educational Laboratory.

Palincsar, A. S., & Brown, A. L. (1984). Reciprocal teaching of comprehension fostering and comprehension monitoring activities. *Cognition and Instruction, 2,* 117–175.

Palincsar, A. S., & Brown, A. L. (1986). Interactive teaching to promote independent learning from text. *The Reading Teacher, 39*(8), 771–777.

Paris, S. C., & Paris, A. H. (2001). Classroom applications of research on self-regulated learning. *Educational Psychologist, 36*(2), 89–101.

Pressley, M., & Woloshyn, V. (1995). Cognitive strategy instruction that really improves children's academic performance (2nd ed.). Cambridge, MA: Brookline Books.

Pugalee, D. K. (2002). Beyond numbers: Communicating in math class. *ENC Focus, 9*(2), 29–32.

RAND Reading Study Group. (2002). *Reading for understanding: Toward an R&D program in reading comprehension.* Retrieved from www.rand.org/publications.html

Rasinski, T. V. (2000). Speed does matter in reading. *The Reading Teacher, 54,* 146–150.

Rosenshine, B., & Meister, C. (1994, April). A comparison of results with standardized tests and experimenter-developed comprehension tests when teaching cognitive strategies. Paper presented at the annual meeting of the American Educational Research Association, New Orleans.

Samuels, S. J. (2002). Reading fluency: Its development and assessment. In Pacific Resources for Education and Learning (Ed.), *Readings on fluency for "A focus on fluency forum."* Honolulu, HI: PREL.

Saunders, W. M. (2001). Improving literacy achievement for English learners in transitional bilingual programs. In R. E. Slavin & M. Calderón (Eds.), *Effective programs for Latino students* (pp. 171–206). Mahwah, NJ: Lawrence Erlbaum.

Saunders, W., & Goldenberg, C. (1999). Effects of instructional conversations and literature logs on limited and fluent English proficient students' story comprehension and thematic understanding. *Elementary School Journal, 99*(4), 277–301.

Schunk, D. H., & Cox, P. D. (1986). Strategy training and attributional feedback with learning disabled students. *Journal of Educational Psychology, 78,* 201–209.

Schunk, D. H., & Swartz, C. W. (1993). Goals and progressive feedback: Effects on self-efficacy and writing achievement. *Contemporary Educational Psychology, 18,* 337–354.

Shanahan, T. (2002, November). *A sin of the second kind: The neglect of fluency instruction and what we can do about it.* PowerPoint presentation at A Focus on Fluency Forum, San Francisco, CA. Retrieved from http://www.prel.org/programs/rel/fluency/Shanahan.ppt

Shanahan, T. (2017). Disciplinary literacy: The basics. Shanahan on Literacy blog. Posted March 15, 2017 http://shanahanonliteracy.com/blog? page=3

Sharan, S., & Hertz-Lazarowitz, R. (1982). Effects of an instructional change program on teachers' behavior, attitudes and perceptions. *The Journal of Applied Behavioral Science, 18*(2), 185–201.

Short, D., & Fitzsimmons, S. (2007). *Double the work: Challenges and solutions to acquiring language and academic literacy for adolescent English language learners.* A report to Carnegie Corporation of New York. Washington, DC: Alliance for Excellent Education.

Short, E. J., & Ryan, E. B. (1984). Metacognitive differences between skilled and less skilled readers: Remediating deficits through story grammar and attribution training. *Journal of Educational Psychology, 76,* 225–235.

Slavin, R. E. (1980). Cooperative learning. *Review of Educational Research, 2*(50), 241–271.

Slavin, R. E., & Calderón, M. (Eds.) (2001). *Effective programs for Latino students.* Mahwah, NJ: Lawrence Erlbaum.

Slavin, R. E., & Cheung, A. (2004). How do English language learners learn to read? *Educational Leadership, 61*(6), 52–57.

Slavin, R. E., & Madden, N. A. (1999). Effects of bilingual and English as second language adaptations of Success for All on the reading achievement of students acquiring English. *Journal of Education for Students Placed at Risk, 4*(4), 393–416.

Slavin, R. E., & Madden, N. A. (2001). *One million children: Success for all.* Thousand Oaks, CA: Corwin.

Slavin, R. E., Madden, N., Calderón, M., Chamberlain, A., & Hennessy, M. (2009). *Fifth-year reading and language outcomes of a randomized evaluation of transitional bilingual education: Report to IES.* Washington, DC: Institute for Education Sciences, U.S. Department of Education.

Snow, C., Burns, S., & Griffin, P. (1998). *Preventing reading difficulties in young children.* Washington, DC: National Academy Press.

Spanier, B. (1992). Encountering the biological sciences: Ideology, language, and learning. In A. Herrington & C. Moran (Eds.), *Writing, teaching, and learning in the disciplines* (pp. 193–212). New York, NY: Modern Language Association.

Sparks, D., & Hirsh, S. (1997). *A new vision for staff development.* Alexandria, VA: ASCD.

Sparks, S. (2017, May 17). Children must be taught to collaborate. *EDWEEK.*

Stevens, R. J., Slavin, R. E., & Farnish, A. M. (1991). The effects of cooperative learning and direct instruction in reading comprehension strategies on main idea identification. *Journal of Educational Psychology, 83*(1), 8–16.

Taylor, B. M., & Beach, R. W. (1984). Effects of text structure instruction on middle-grade students' comprehension and production of expository text. *Reading Research Quarterly, 19*(2), 147–161.

Taylor, B. M., Pearson, P. D., Peterson, D. S., & Rodriguez, M. C. (2003). Reading growth in high-poverty classrooms: The influence of teacher practices that encourage cognitive engagement in literacy learning. *Elementary School Journal, 104,* 3–28.

Tharp, R. G., & Yamauchi, L. A. (1994). Effective instructional conversation in Native American classrooms. *Center for Research on Education, Diversity and Excellence,* Paper EPR10.

Tierney, R. J., & Readence, J. E. (2000). *Reading strategies and practices: A compendium* (5th ed.). Boston, MA: Allyn and Bacon.

Torgesen, J. K., Rashotte, C. A., Alexander, A. W., Alexander, J., & McFee, K. (2002, November). *The challenge of fluent reading for older children with reading difficulties.* PowerPoint presentation at A Focus on Fluency Forum, San Francisco, CA. Retrieved from http://www.prel.org/programs/rel/fluency/Torgesen.ppt

Tschannen-Moran, M., & Barr, M. (2004). Fostering student achievement: The relationship between collective teacher efficacy and student achievement. *Leadership and Policy in Schools, 3,* 187–207.

Valdéz, G. (1996). *Con respeto.* New York: Teachers College Press.

Williams, J. (2010). Taking on the role of questioner: Revisiting reciprocal teaching. *The Reading Teacher, 64*(4), 278–281.

Zimmerman, B. J., Bonner, S., & Kovach, R. (1996). *Developing self-regulated learners: Beyond achievement to self-efficacy.* Washington, DC: American Psychological Association.

ADDITIONAL RESOURCES

Calderón, M. E. (2007). *Teaching reading to English language learners, Grades 6–12: A framework for improving achievement in the content areas.* Thousand Oaks, CA: Corwin.

Calderón, M. E. (2007). *RIGOR! Reading Instructional Goals for Older Readers: Reading program for 6th-12th students with interrupted formal education.* New York: Benchmark Education Co.

Calderón, M. E. (2016, February). A whole-school approach to English Learners. In *Educational Leadership* Online Journal, *73*(5). Alexandria, VA: ASCD.

Calderón, M., August, D., & Minaya-Rowe, L. (2004). *ExC-ELL: Expediting comprehension for English-language learners.* New York, NY: Carnegie Corporation of New York.

Calderón, M., & Cummins, J. (1982). *Communicative competence in bilingual education: Theory and research.* Dallas, TX: National Center for the Development of Bilingual Curriculum.

Joyce, B., & Showers, B. (2002). *Student achievement through staff development* (3rd ed.). Alexandria, VA: ASCD.

Lazarowitz, R., & Karsenty. G. (1990). Cooperative learning and students' academic achievement, process skills, learning environment, and self-esteem in tenth grade biology classrooms. In S. Sharan (Ed.), *Cooperative learning: Theory and research* (pp. 123–149). New York, NY: Praeger.

Moir, E., & Bloom, G. (2003). Fostering leadership through mentoring. *Educational Leadership, 60*(8), 58–61.

Nagy, W. (2005). Why vocabulary instruction needs to be long-term and comprehensive. In E. H. Hiebert & M. L. Kamil (Eds.), *Teaching and learning vocabulary: Bringing research to practice* (pp. 27–44). Mahwah, NJ: Lawrence Erlbaum.

National Panel on Literacy for Adolescent English Language Learners. (2006). *Double the work: Academic literacy for adolescent English language learners.* New York, NY: Carnegie Corporation of New York.

Bloom's Taxonomy: https://cft.vanderbilt.edu/guides-sub-pages/blooms-taxonomy/

Effects of Bilingual Cooperative Integrated Reading and Composition: www.journals.uchicago.edu/doi/abs/10.1086/461920

www.all4ed.org

www.nassp.org

www.carnegie.org

www.corestandards.org/ELA-Literacy/W/7/

Index

A SAGE Publishing Company

CORWIN HAS ONE MISSION: to enhance education through intentional professional learning.

We build long-term relationships with our authors, educators, clients, and associations who partner with us to develop and continuously improve the best evidence-based practices that establish and support lifelong learning.

Solutions you want. Experts you trust.
Results you need.

AUTHOR
CONSULTING

Author Consulting

On-site professional learning with sustainable results! Let us help you design a professional learning plan to meet the unique needs of your school or district. www.corwin.com/pd

INSTITUTES

Institutes

Corwin Institutes provide collaborative learning experiences that equip your team with tools and action plans ready for immediate implementation. www.corwin.com/institutes

ECOURSES

eCourses

Practical, flexible online professional learning designed to let you go at your own pace. www.corwin.com/ecourses

READ2EARN

Read2Earn

Did you know you can earn graduate credit for reading this book? Find out how: www.corwin.com/read2earn

Contact an account manager at (800) 831-6640 or visit **www.corwin.com** for more information.